BEHOLD A GIANT

THE STORY OF A WINDMILL

THE WINDMILL

By Henry Wadsworth Longfellow

Behold! A giant am I!
Aloft here in my tower,
With my granite jaws I devour
The maize, and the wheat, and the rye,
And grind them into flour.

I look down over the farms;
In the fields of grain I see
The harvest that is to be,
And I fling to the air my arms,
For I know it is all for me.

I hear the sound of flails
Far off, from the threshing-floors
In barns, with their open doors,
And the wind, the wind in my sails,
Louder and louder roars.

I stand here in my place,
With my foot on the rock below,
And whichever way it may blow
I meet it face to face,
As a brave man meets his foe.

And while we wrestle and strive,
My master, the miller, stands
And feeds me with his hands;
For he knows who makes him thrive,
Who makes him lord of lands

On Sundays I take my rest;
Church-going bells begin
Their low, melodious din;
I cross my arms on my breast,
And all is peace within.

First Published in 2012 by A & G Swift Publishers.
81 Gravelly Bank, Lightwood, Stoke-on-Trent, Staffordshire ST3 7EF

Text – Gillian Hudson Swift.

ISBN 0-978-0-9550556-1-4

Publishers A & G Swift

Typeset & Printed by Sherwin Rivers Ltd, Waterloo Road, Cobridge, Stoke-on-Trent, Staffordshire, ST6 3HR

FOREWORD

The Foreword to this book has been written by Henry Sandon MBE, who is a well-known authority concerning Worcester porcelain. He is highly regarded in the UK for his many appearances on the Antiques Road Show. In 2008 he agreed to be Patron of the Meir Heath Preservation Group due to his interest in matters historical.

BEHOLD A GIANT
– THE STORY OF A WINDMILL

Meir Heath Windmill has stood silent sentinel, watching over its village of that name since 1775. A giant of a building, then much higher than the few surrounding cottages, it has remained, battered by wind, rain and snow and occasionally enjoying sunshine.

The Windmill Tower is a Grade II listed building and was declared to be 'At Risk' by Stafford Borough Council.

Local residents have shown interest in its use as a present-day landmark as well as its previous use as a wind-driven corn mill.

A local delicacy, the North Staffordshire oatcake, probably gave it much work in days gone by, although it was a general mill, grinding oats, wheat and barley.

It is known that the miller brewed beer at the Mill House, the building at the top of Grindley Lane.

A multitude of archivists, museum curators, senior citizens and curious school children have all had their say in this account of the history of Meir Heath Windmill.

All this evidence has been skilfully woven into this story of the mill, its history and the struggle to save it for future generations, for it is only by knowledge of the past that we understand the present.

When I was a lad, I lived in Soho in the shadow of the Windmill Theatre, which stands on the site of the great mill that ground the corn for London. The theatre never closed during the war and stands as a symbol for the majestic structure from which it takes its name.

I am proud to have been invited to write the Foreword to such a book, written by so keen a group as the Meir Heath Windmill Preservation Group.

Henry Sandon MBE

INFORMATION ABOUT THE PROJECT MANAGER

Mrs G Swift is the Secretary and Project Manager. A retired primary school teacher, she taught for 35 years and was a middle school governor for ten years. A keen historian and collector of old documents, Mrs Swift went on to write a local history book about Fenton and Crown Staffs pottery.

Doing this, she interviewed people and collected their memories, and had experience of using oral history methods.

Over the years, as Secretary of the group, she has taken 12 of its members into three local schools to talk to the children about the Windmill Project and during the next few months is planning to go into local schools with displays and talks concerning learning in the project.

Mrs Swift organised the group to become a Company Limited by Guarantee and a Charity and does all the communications concerning Companies House.

Mrs Swift is also the Secretary of the local Shooters Hill History Group.

**Gillian Hudson Swift,
the Secretary/Project Manager**

THE HISTORY OF A WINDMILL & ITS LOCALITY
BY GILLIAN HUDSON SWIFT SUPPORTED BY MEIR HEATH WINDMILL PRESERVATION GROUP

Chairman Mr Anthony Swift
Treasurer Mrs Dorothy M. Bestwick
Secretary & Project Manager Mrs Gillian Swift

Directors

Dame Maureen Upton   Mr John Upton   Mrs Mary Flannagan

Mr Nigel Morley   Mrs Dorothy M. Bestwick   Mr Anthony Swift

Mrs Gillian Swift

Committee Members

Mr Peter Lawton   Mr Roy Deakin   Mr Alfred Oakes

Miss Brenda Smith   Mrs Sharon Beardmore   Mr David Beardmore

Mrs Sylvia Ebrill   Mr George Ebrill   Mrs Nita Mould

Mr Clive Mould

Company number 5835854   Charity number 1115772

**Windmill Group 2006 – A Mountford, J Bradbeer, G Swift, A Swift, R Deakin,
N Morley P Lawton, D Jones, A Oakes, M Flannagan, J Upton and M Upton**

ACKNOWLEDGEMENTS

Her Majesty the Queen

Patron: Henry Sandon MBE

Mike O'Keefe at Royal Images

Christopher Sandamas, Chief Clerk to Her Majesty the Queen

Ian White, Solicitor, Knights, Newcastle-under-Lyme

Martin Levie, Architect, Harrison Wood

Phil Hancock, Mrs Karen Hancock and Mr N J Clowes, Hodson Builders

Councillor Ian Parry, Staffordshire County Council

Penny McKnight, Senior Conservation Officer, Stafford Borough Council

Susie Empsall, Planning Officer, Staffordshire Borough Council

John Boucher, Consultant, Millwrights

B Hall, Head teacher (retired), Sandon Business and Enterprise College

P Marsden, Sandon Business and Enterprise College

Celia Shemilt

Eileen Hallam

Peter Siddley, Head teacher (retired), Meir Heath Primary School

Bernadette Malvern, Head teacher (retired), Springcroft Primary School, Blythe Bridge

Simon Mottram, Meir Heath Primary School

Voluntary Action Stoke-on-Trent

Terry Walsh, Radio Stoke

Stafford District Voluntary Services, Catherine Anderson and Laura McDonald

Grassroots Community Fund

Staffordshire Environmental Fund

Ibstock Cory Trust

Awards for All

Target Windows

David Swift: Meir Heath Windmill website: www.meirheathwindmill.co.uk

Lisa Swift, Windmill Treasure Hunt Boards

Maureen and John Upton, and St John's Ambulance, Stafford

Mary Evans, Estate Manager, M&B Company; Shaun Darley, Director, Property, M&B Company; John Fairbanks, Windmill Expert; Adam Hill, Head of Leisure, Stafford Borough Council; Midland Wind and Water Mills Group; Dorothy, Andrew and Richard Bestwick; Councillor Elaine Philpott; Mark Beardmore; Clive and Nita Mould; Roy Deakin; Peter Lawton; Alfred Oakes; Brenda Smith; Sharon and David Beardmore; Sylvia and George Ebrill; John Bradbeer; Mary Flannagan; Nigel Morley; Robin Bagnall; Judith and Richard Cresswell; John Banks; Antony, Joanne and Josh Mitchell-Waite; Don and Jen Mason; Ann Charnock; Alan Mountford; Tom and Chris Preston; Liz Shaw; John Dutton; Barbara Wild; Liz Reynolds; Hilary Huson; Margaret Leach; John and Lynn Kocierz; Glynn Thursfield; Barry and Maureen Shaw; Howard and Linda Platt; Leslie Bartlam; John and Dawn Mason; Heather Gordon; Bruce Barker; William Keeling; Di and Michelle Halket; Mick and Michelle Wild; Jean Hughes; Oliver and James Deakin; Rita and David Deakin; and Emma Khaleela.

Annual General Meeting (2006) at Florence Sports and Social Club –
D Jones, P Lawton, N Morley, J Upton, J Bradbeer, A Mountford, M Upton,
M Flannagan, G Swift, A Swift and D Bestwick

CONTENTS

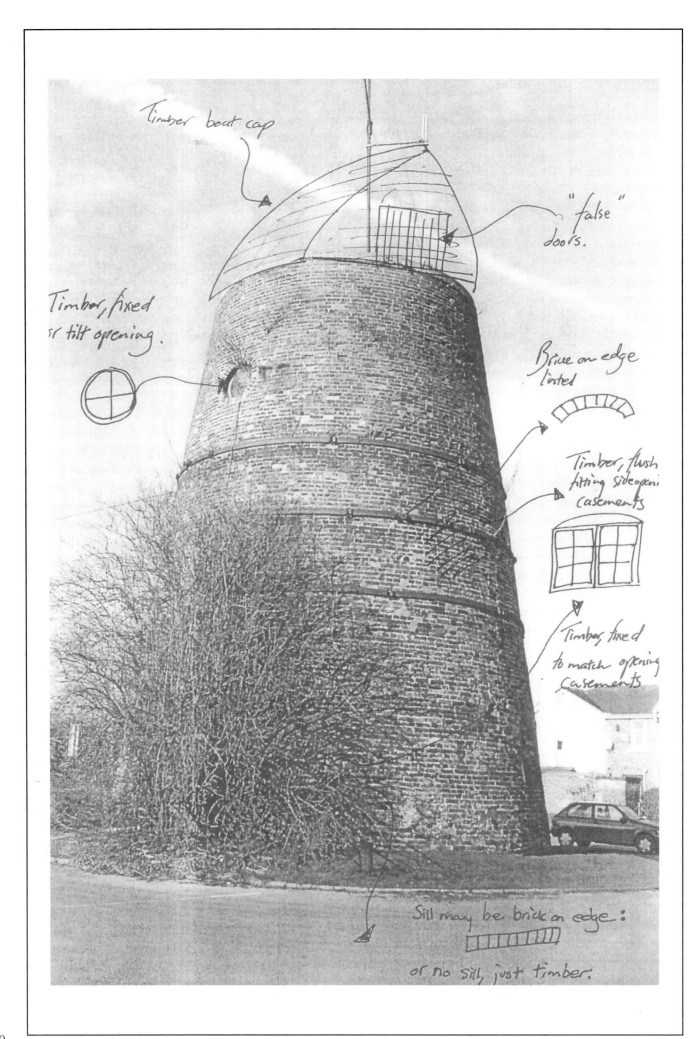

Timber boat cap

"false" doors.

Timber, fixed or tilt opening.

Brice on edge lintel

Timber, flush fitting sideopeni casements

Timber, fixed to match opening casements

Sill may be brick on edge: or no sill, just timber.

outsucken *The freedom of a tenant from bondage to a mill; or the liberty which he enjoys by his lease of taking his grain to be ground where he pleases.*

THE HISTORY OF A WINDMILL

The Windmill

By Henry Wadsworth Longfellow
Behold! A giant am I,
Aloft here in my tower,
With my granite jaws I devour
The maize, and the wheat, and the rye,
And grind them into flour.

Meir Heath Windmill History Chart

Date	Event
2010	• *New boat cap fixed to the tower* • *Two green oak beams fixed at the top of the tower*
2009	• *Old beams removed (rotten)* • *New doors and windows fixed* • *Hatch formed with concertina ladder*
2008	• *Architect consulted and plans drawn*
2007	• *Solicitor Ian White (Knights, Newcastle-under-Lyme) joins the group*
2006	• *The Group becomes a Company Limited by Guarantee*
2006	• *The Group becomes a Charity*
2004	• *Meir Heath Windmill Group formed*
1960	• *The Watch Tower taken off the roof of the mill* • *Radio communication aerials put on to the top of the windmill*
1939	• *The windmill still had cap and sails Home Guard removed the sails, and mill was used as a watch tower*
1928	• *Mill used as a water tower* • *It was bought by Joules Brewery*
1914	• *Alton's sold The Dusty Miller public house*
1908	• *Staffordshire Potteries Water WorksnWater tank installed for local distribution of water*
1908	• *Alton's Brewery from Derby acquired the windmill and The Dusty Miller public house*
1881	• *Census - Who lived at the windmill and Dusty Miller*
1775	• *Windmill seen on Yates' map*

G Swift, A Mountford, A Swift, N Morley, M Flannagan,
A Oakes, H Huson, P Lawton and R Deakin

The Windmill Tower & Dusty Miller public house
(By kind permission of Stafford Record Office)

The Windmill Inn showing Joules sign

The Situation of the Windmill

Meir Heath Windmill is shown on the map and is at a junction of five important roads. The B5029 Grindley Lane to Blythe Bridge and Cheadle, the B5066 to Hilderstone, the A520 to Rough Close and Stone, the A520 to Leek and Common Lane. The Hilderstone Road to Sandon was a turnpike road and had a toll house near to the windmill. The Meir Heath Windmill was first seen on a Yates map, we believe, in 1775. This is the earliest record we could find with information about the windmill.

The Windmill (1902)

Yates' Map of Staffordshire

The map we had a copy of was a Yates map, which was copied on a visit to meet a lady called Sylvia Adams. She heard us asking to see the Yates Map of 1775 Staffordshire and she said that Thomas Yates was her grandfather x3. Sylvia said that Thomas Yates came from Stowe by Chartley. As we spoke about the famous Yates family, Sylvia told us that Thomas's name appeared at the bottom of the 1775 map as the seller. She thinks that he could have been an assistant to William in the survey. After her research, she found that Thomas Yates spent some time in Liverpool with William Yates.

William Yates (1738–1802) cartographer, Thomas Yates land surveyor

In 2012, Sylvia sent me a copy of the William Yates geodetic survey. It is interesting to see Meir Heath Windmill on the north-south axis from Yates' triangulation. Sylvia sent us an interesting item which was information from the Birmingham Gazette, 31 January 1780. The title was 'Survey of Staffordshire on 1st March 1780 will be published'. It went on to say that the Second Impression of Messrs William & Thomas Yates' Survey of Staffordshire was laid down to the true geometric situation of every market town, village seat, park of nobility, and gentry, main roads, crossroads, Roman roads, toll roads and mile stones. It went on to say that also shown were inns, farms, woods, mountains, lakes, ponds, rivers, brooks and canals with wharf and locks. Mentioned were Needwood Forest and Cannock Chase, land that was common or waste land, unenclosed at the time of the survey. It was interesting to read that the latitude and longitude meridian lines were accurately ascertained and astronomically observed. The information went on to state that it was "elegantly engraved on a scale of one inch to one mile and that it would be delivered to the purchaser in six sheets at £1 1s 0d or could be pasted upon canvas and coloured at £1 11s & 6d". We are just remembering pounds shillings and pence. The map could be bought at Pearsons Rollinsons in Birmingham, Mr Williams in Shrewsbury, Morgans in Lichfield, Smarts in Wolverhampton, Smiths in Newcastle and Mr Rays Stationers in Stafford. This map can be seen at Stafford Record Office with an introduction by AD M Phillips (SH64ser xii 1984).

13

Maps

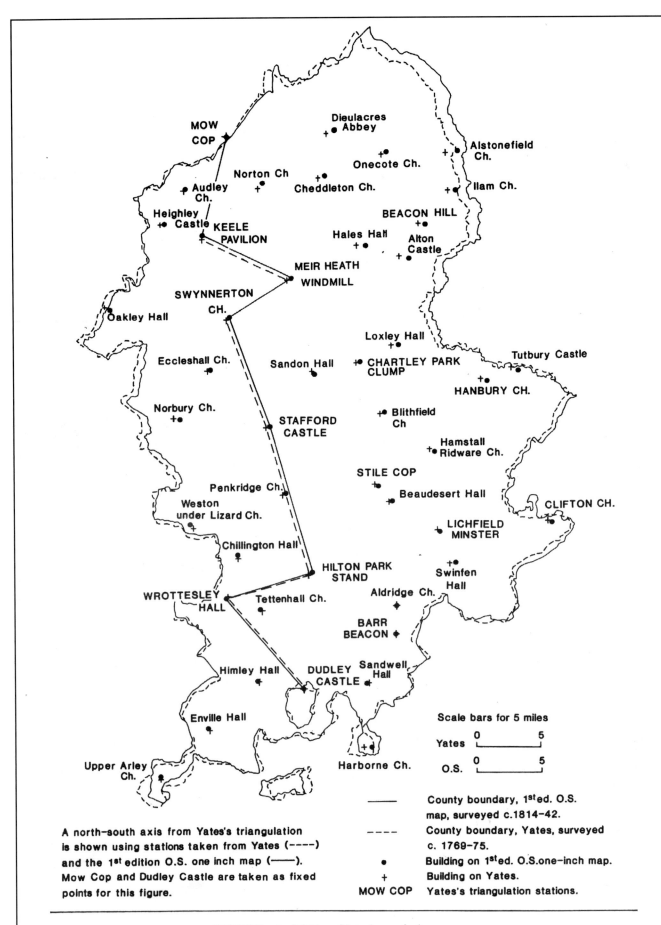

FIGURE 1. William Yates's geodetic survey.

The Windmill Project
- What Happened First?

On 4 March 2007 I received a letter from an officer at Mitchells & Butlers, which stated that it was their intention to effect necessary repairs to the windmill to ensure the structure's integrity. It went on to state that all vegetation growing on the brickwork would be removed and that the rainwater systems would be repaired in the near future.

The Company agreed the scope of the work with Penny McKnight of Staffordshire Borough Council. They also agreed to remove any unnecessary radio equipment from the top of the mill and remove the rubbish in the mill.

They went on to say that they had no intention of restoring or partially reinstating the mill at this time or in the future.

However, once the works outlined above had been executed, they stated that they would be happy to let our group take possession of the mill and reinstate all or part of it.

At the next Committee meeting the group decided to go ahead with the project.

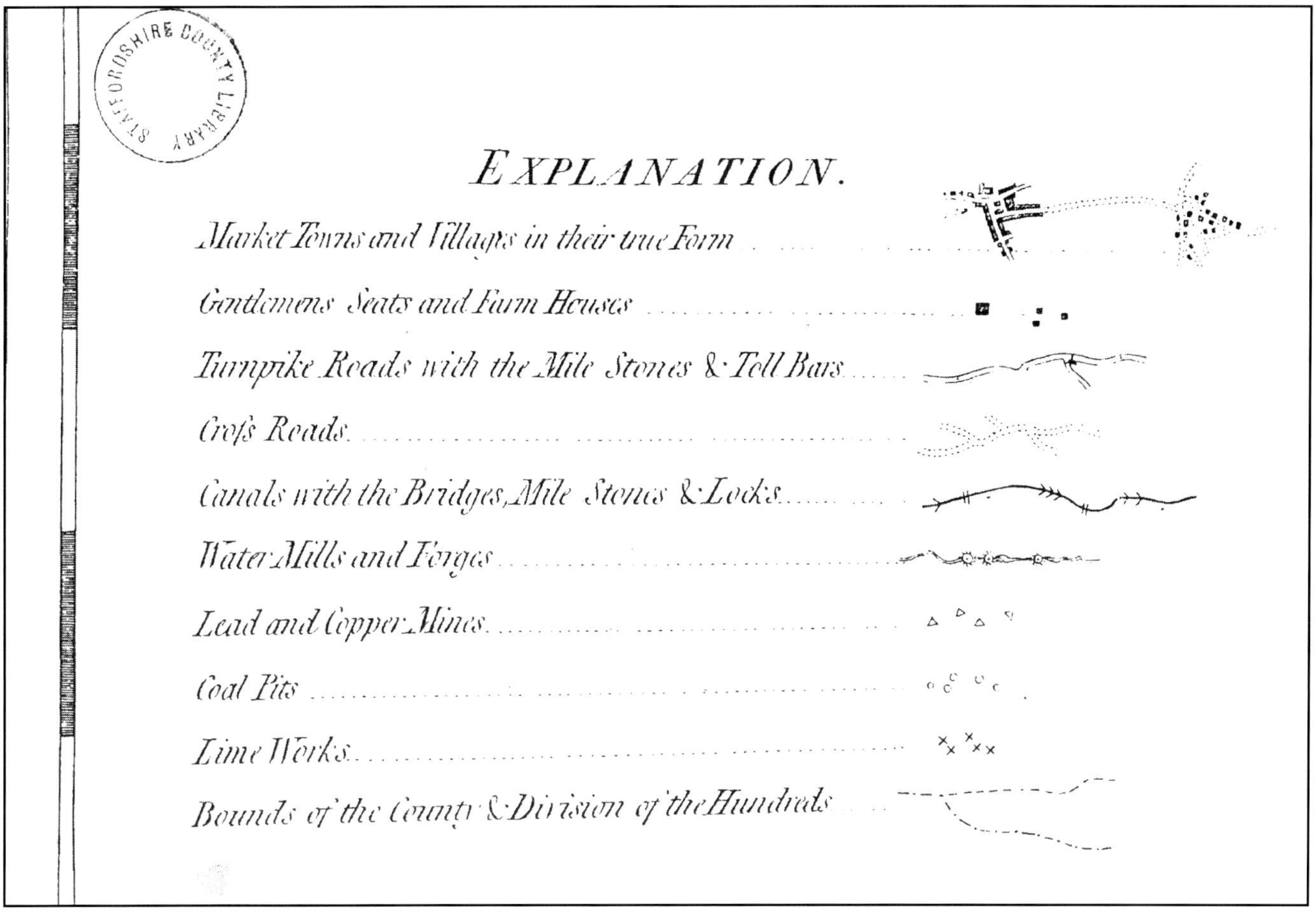

EXPLANATION.

Market Towns and Villages in their true Form

Gentlemens Seats and Farm Houses

Turnpike Roads with the Mile Stones & Toll Bars

Cross Roads

Canals with the Bridges, Mile Stones & Locks

Water Mills and Forges

Lead and Copper Mines

Coal Pits

Lime Works

Bounds of the County & Division of the Hundreds

R Deakin, S Ebrill, G Ebrill, D Bestwick, J Upton, G Swift, A Swift, P Lawton, M Flannagan, C Mould, N Mould
– some of the Committee

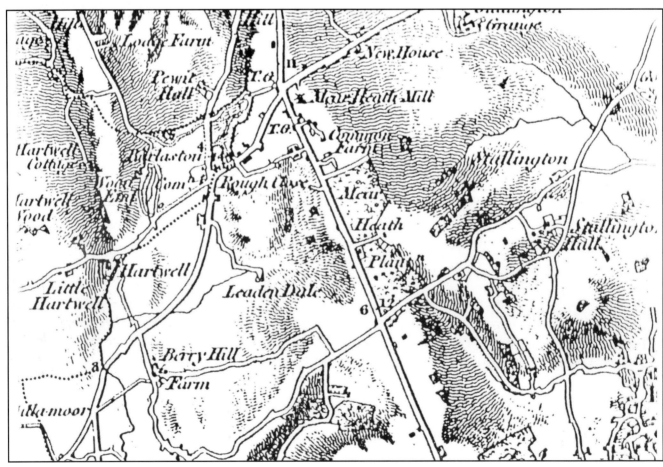

(possibly 1798) Meir Heath Windmill can be seen near the top of the map
(By kind permission of Stafford Record Office)

Letters from Children at Meir Heath Primary School

5 December 2007

Dear Mrs Swift,

I am writing to support the restoration of the windmill, situated on Hilderstone Road, Meir Heath. I think it would be brilliant if the old building was restored to its original state. Everyone at our school is very enthusiastic about the idea.

The windmill means such a lot to us here in Meir Heath. So I really support the idea of restoring it. The windmill also is very important to our school as it is the symbol on our uniforms. The idea of turning it into a museum is a spectacular one. I think that it would be very educational and would attract more visitors to our village.

The windmill being done up would also bring back happy memories to people who had once played in it in past years.

Who would want to remove such a precious piece of local history?

The windmill being restored would be a happy sight for residents of Meir Heath because I can guarantee that they would all love to see the cap and sails on again.

Please read my letter and take in my opinion of the idea.

Yours faithfully

Bethany

Aged 10 exactly

(As it is my Birthday Today! Wednesday 5th December 07)

Dear Sir/Madam

I am writing this letter to save the wonderful Windmill that has been on Hilderstone Road for many centuries. This landmark cannot be knocked down and I strongly agree of what Mrs Swift's history group is trying to achieve.

The children at this school would love the amazing windmill to be a Museum and they said that if it does become one it could teach lots of people about the Windmill when it was old and what it looked inside.

So we all wish that the Windmill can be built up to its normal state of course with a cap on top. Then we could all come to see the Windmill when it's all done and dusted.

If you saw the children at our school you wouldn't believe how much we support the Windmill, we have it on our school cardigans, jumpers and it is also our school logo.

Emma

Email from Glynis Powell, Museums, Libaries and Archives West Midlands, to Gill Swift

Date: 1 December 2006

Subject: Meir Heath Windmill – fundraising

I understand from the message that some help and advice was needed concerning a structural survey for the windmill. As the query was passed to me, I assume it was a query as much about funding possibilities as anything else (I am one of the funding advisers here).

Firstly, you may find if you do not have contact already, that the Museum Development Officer for Staffordshire would be a good general contact to make. She is based at Shugborough. Her job is to support museums and heritage groups throughout the county. She sometimes has small funds available and is always a useful contact for information and making useful connections.

Secondly, MLA does not directly administer very many funds itself. There is a small grant fund called the Service Development Fund, but I don't think, in the case of the Meir Heath Windmill, it would be entirely appropriate. However you are welcome to apply (we are awaiting Board approval for the next round, which is likely to have an application deadline of March 2007).

More positively, I think the project could be looked on kindly by parts of the Heritage Lottery Fund. Awards for All and Your Heritage would both be appropriate – especially with your schools and local community interest and input. For HLF a structural survey would be just part of an application – a means to an end. The regional officers are very supportive and are worth talking to before making an application. If you have already gone down this route, but not been successful, I am more than happy to talk through possible ways of reapplying.

There are also some funds you could try from the architectural heritage fund. Specifically the Options Appraisal Fund http://www.ahfund.org.uk/finance_grants.htm.

As the Windmill is a Grade II listed building you obviously have some contacts with English Heritage. While they tend not to provide funds for Grade II buildings, they should be, in any case, consulted about work done and may be able to give you the name of a local historic surveyor to do the work (who you could ask to do it on a slightly cheaper basis? Always worth asking).

Reply from Gill Swift to Glynis Powell, MLA, West Midlands

A structural survey is needed by Liz Woodhall, Heritage Lottery Fund (HLF). She is very helpful and has been twice to the mill. This year we became a C.L.B.G. and obtained charitable status.

M and B Company offer us a 25-year lease at peppercorn rent. They expect us to pay for their solicitors as well as ours – £1,000.

The group think it would be sensible to get a structural survey done before accepting a lease. Mr J Boucher, Millwright, came and spent two hours inspecting the mill. He sent the enclosed report. HLF wouldn't consider paying for a boat cap or sails. They will consider repairs to floors inside and making a Heritage Centre (possible on outside walls). I have contacted Helen Johnson. I have contacted Penny McKnight, Conservation Officer Stafford Borough Council; Lisa Heaton, Stafford Borough Council. She gave us your address and English Heritage.

Gisela from English Heritage (EH) sent a list of engineers for us to contact. She said that EH were not interested in helping Grade II (How do we get to Grade I?) Local Parish Council, Fulford, gave us £250 to help us run the group. John Gifford (Pro help Birmingham can't help) Awards for All said No because I put whole project … they only go to £25,000. Liz said that I should get back to Awards for All and try and negotiate. I have looked at so many websites.

Staffordshire Voluntary Action sent me FUND RAISERS (20), the Committee wrote to them, all said no to building work. I will see what the seminar offers. Money is tight and the local council gave last year, so will not give this year. I would like to talk to you. Yours is the most encouraging email I have had in a long time.

All the group are disappointed with no way to move forward. We seem to be stuck on this survey. We have been trying to save the mill since Dec 2004. The Company who owns it would not cooperate at all the first year so we have moved on that score. We continue with fundraising events.

Supporters

Our group contacted many people to get their support and one who wrote back promptly was John Fairbanks.

Here are extracts from a letter from John Fairbanks, Fairbanks Complete Funeral Services, Stone, to Gill Swift regarding Meir Heath Windmill Restoration Project.

I have been giving a lot more thought on how best to guide you in tackling this wonderful project. The following may be of some help on seeing a gradual progress and a way forward once you have secure occupation of the site as a trust or whatever.

You have had the assistance, I hope, of a good legal practice to set up the trust to ensure that the brewery gives you your head to do up and run the project properly with, I would hope, some financial input from them as when the project is completed they will be receiving an increase in the bar takings for food and drink. The site will attract a lot more visitors than can be realised at the moment.

I have seen inside the mill and would consider that the tower can be scaffolded from top to bottom inside the tower from the concrete slab at first-floor level. This scaffolding will remain in place for some considerable time, only being removed as the two floors above and upright shaft have been fixed with its associated gearing.

… As regards the Meir Heath Windmill, I can only say that this is the most worthwhile project that has come to life for many a while.

This is a subject I do know something about having worked in a few and manufactured, supplied and fitted new sails.

Meir Heath mill had two pairs of common sails and was kept into the wind by a tail pole and winch. The mill had two doors on the ground floor to allow access when the wind was in an unfavourable direction. The sails were 60 feet in diameter with the tip of the sail just clearing the mound. To operate the sails the mill would be pulled out of the wind for the miller to climb up the sails to furl or unfurl the sail cloth. A bit of a dodgy job, which the advent of spring-shuttered sails and patent sails eliminated.

At the top of the tower a series of beams some 8 feet long are in the brickwork to which the cap curb is fixed. On this curb the cap rotates.

I have never seen inside the mill but would welcome the opportunity to see if any of the main beams remain to bear witness to the position of the mechanism.

Look forward to hearing from you. J Fairbanks

Meir Heath Primary School OFSTED Inspection (6–10 June 2005)

Mr Peter Siddley sent our group a copy of the OFSTED report that mentioned our group visiting the school to help pupils understand the past.

Mr Peter Siddley, head teacher of Meir Heath Primary School, asked if our group would go in and talk to the children during the OFSTED inspection about the local area and WWII. We did and the inspectors were pleased to see us there.

Extract from report – Humanities

History and geography were sampled and no overall judgements about provision were made. The school enhances its provision in these subjects well through educational visits, and teachers plan effectively to provide first-hand experiences to support pupils' learning. These experiences help to bring the subjects alive and contribute well to developing pupils' understanding of the world around them and of what happened in the past. During the inspection, pupils in Year 5 made very good progress in understanding about life during World War II as they interviewed local elderly residents about their experiences and memories. Pupils were highly motivated by the experience that imprinted many facts indelibly on their minds.

Stafford District Voluntary Services

We have received a lot of useful advice from the officers of the Stafford District Voluntary Services (SDVS) and are very grateful for all their help.

Letter from Helen Dart, SDVS, to Anthony Swift (5 July 2006)

I am very pleased to inform you that at its recent meeting the Executive Committee of Stafford District Voluntary Services accepted the application of Meir Heath Windmill Preservation Group to be admitted to membership of SDVS and has entered your organisation on the Register of Members, your membership number is 119. Enclosed are a copy of our most recent Annual Review and a copy of our most recent newsletter – Network. For further information please access our website at www.sdvs.org.uk. Matt Hancock will be contacting you shortly for more information about your organisation so that we can enter your details in our Directory if you wish. New members are encouraged to write an article about their organisation so that it can be published in our bi-monthly newsletter. Please contact Matt Hancock at matt@sdvs.org.uk or telephone 606670, if you would like to submit an article.

If there is any way that we can be of assistance to your organisation please do not hesitate to contact me.

Meir Heath Windmill – The Future

The Committee invited the Head of Leisure at Stafford Borough Council to look at the mill to see if the council might help to save it from further deterioration. This report was sent to the Committee in 2006.

Meir Heath is recognised not only as a landmark for the area but also has a degree of historic relevance to the area in terms of local history. However, as you are very much aware, the condition of the mill is poor and although some health and safety work has been undertaken to ensure the structural

integrity is sound, this has not stopped the deterioration of the mill.

Our inspection and subsequent review has identified water ingress around the flat roof area, penetrating into the timbers, which also showed signs of wet rot passing down into the brickwork coursing. It was also noted that general movement has and may still be occurring in the top third of the tower, which can be visibly seen by the inclining inwards of the brickwork. It has also been identified that the concrete cap has degraded to the point of becoming porous.

The site itself is also a difficult one, in terms of gaining approval from the brewery in terms of access, car parking and the fact it is situated on private land, with practically no surrounding land belonging to the mill or as it appears, no chance of any land being offered up by the brewery as part of the transfer. There is also an issue regarding access to power.

It is estimated that re-instatement of the mill could be in the region of £300,000 excluding any operating and day-to-day costs. Unfortunately the authority is not in a position to be able to underwrite this level of cost.

I am, however, supportive of what you are trying to achieve and am happy to offer guidance in relation to the positive things that can be undertaken and, where possible, offer officer time and expertise to assist you in obtaining funding or linking through to specialist knowledge as your project develops.

The Committee were happy to know that Stafford Borough Council offered its help.

The Windmill Inn

Ernest Gimbert and his wife Fanny had the Windmill Inn when Joules were providing the beer. The Badderley family are relations of Julia Jackson (née Gimbert) and her parents John and Nora Gimbert.

Nora's Bar

We Tried Everything to Get Help for the Windmill Project

In 2005 the Committee decided to apply to the BBC Endemol Restoration programme to see if we could get a grant from them.

BBC Endemol Restoration – A new development (March 2006)

In December 2005, the Secretary sent information regarding the Windmill to BBC Endemol programme researchers, explaining the mill was in danger of being lost to our community. Two weeks ago the Secretary heard from them and they are interested but need more details.

The Secretary thought it would be of interest for M&B to know that the Endemol Company at the BBC was showing this interest. The Man from the BBC rang twice last week to ask why there was a delay in the brewery carrying out repairs to the roof, the water ingress, and the bulge in the wall and correcting the pointing. All this was agreed last year with Stafford Borough Council Conservation Officer.

The Secretary pointed out to him that Mitchells and Butlers had taken down aerials, removed rubbish, a tree stump and cut the grass, thus showing good will on the part of the brewery. Endemol also wished to see the feasibility study, which has been sent. Of course, the water getting in is of great concern to the group and everyone involved. If the BBC do ask to film the Windmill and M&B are kind enough to give their permission, it could be very good publicity for M&B Brewery.

BBC Radio Stoke has asked if our group will do a programme about our progress and endeavours and we intend to do that quite soon. It could be a wonderful project on an endangered building if everyone cooperated.

Our Group members were all delighted at the interest shown. Our hopes were raised.

Sadly some weeks later we heard that another windmill was to be supported by Endemol. We were refused help because we didn't have a lease.

The Midland Wind and Water Mills Group

The Midland Wind and Water Mills Group have been very supportive. Our members enjoy the magazines they produce and we were grateful for the donation of £250.

Excerpt from a Letter from Tony Perryer, Midland Wind & Water Mills Group, to Gill Swift (February 2006)

Thank you very much for your letter of 7th February, your cheque for £8.00 and the copy of Stafford Borough Council's letter.

Firstly, I am pleased to confirm that the Meir Heath Windmill Group has now been registered as a member of the Midland Mills Group. All correspondence will be addressed to you and I would like to welcome you and your Group to our membership.

I enclose a copy of our last Newsletter and am arranging for the Group's Annual Journal, which was issued last April, to be sent to you. You will of course be sent future copies of these publications.

If you or any of your members can get to our winter meetings, you would be most welcome.

In your letter you mention contacting two of our members who, as far as I know, are as knowledgeable as anyone about windmill renovation – Alan Gifford and John Boucher. I will of course keep our Committee informed about your Group but I do recommend that you contact Society for Protection of Ancient Buildings.

Our group were delighted to receive help from such an important group as the Midland Wind and Water Mills Group

**Ernest and Julia Gimbert on a tandem with Nora
and Fanny Badderley** *(All by kind permission of J Jackson)*

**Preservation Group with Awards for All certificate –
M Flannagan, N Morley, A Mountford, P Lawton, D Bestwick, D Jones, G Swift, R Deakin and A Swift**

John Fairbanks

Letter from J Fairbanks to Alan Taylor, English Heritage West Midlands (March 2006)

It is many years now since we discussed mills together and I wish to bring to your attention the Windmill at Meir Heath.

I was approached some 12 months ago by a group of people who wished to see the windmill restored. I went along and gave them a talk and a rough idea of costs. They have now asked me for more details to go forward with a scheme. The enclosure will say more of what it is about. I am only advising but do consider this to be a worthy project. Could you please contact Mrs Swift as I am sure your wisdom can be of assistance to her?

At this time our group needed support and John Fairbanks was one of the best

Notice Board outside mill

supporte

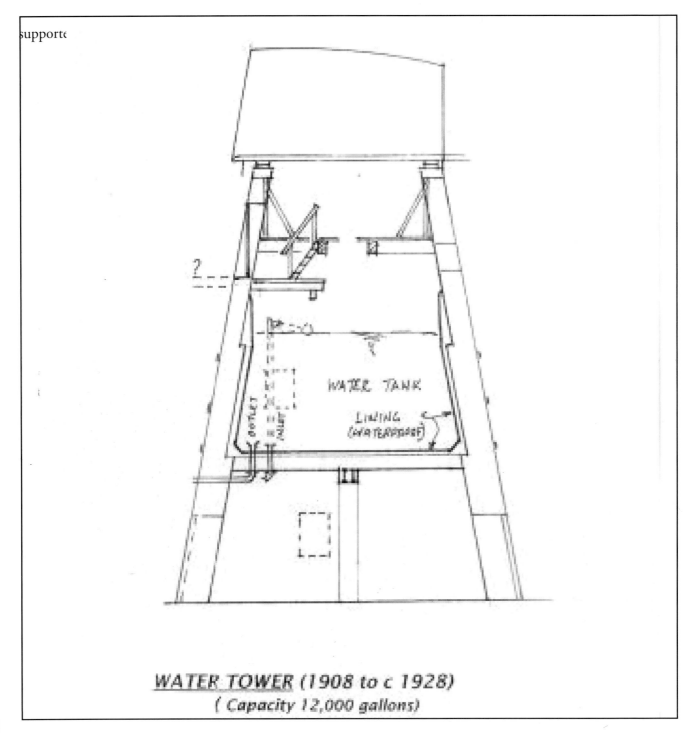

WATER TOWER (1908 to c 1928)
(Capacity 12,000 gallons)

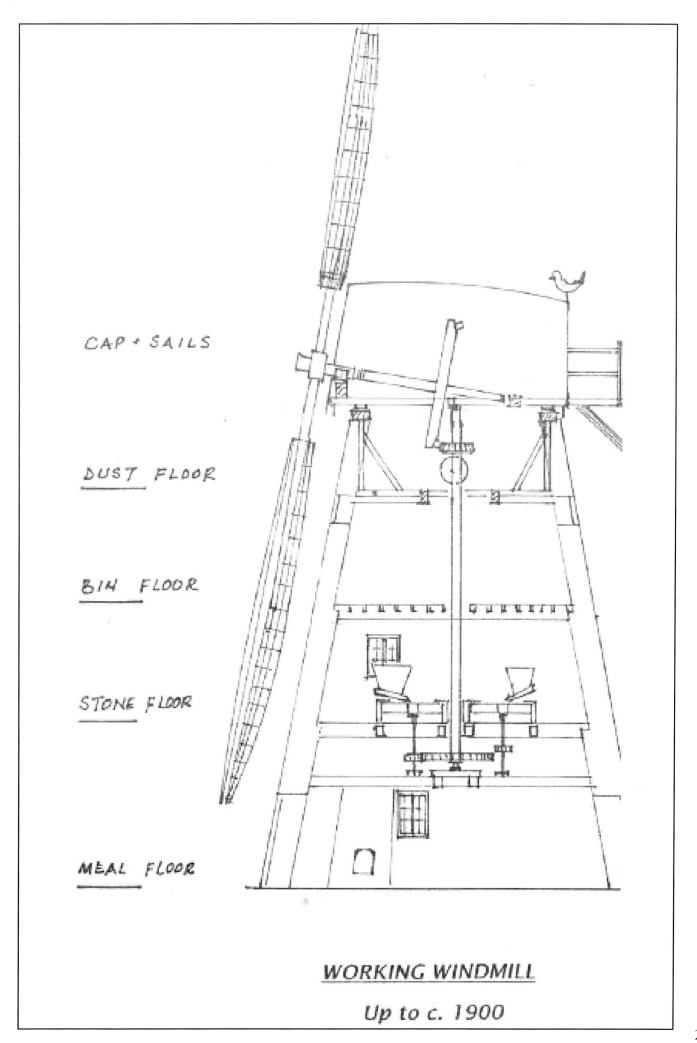

CAP + SAILS

DUST FLOOR

BIN FLOOR

STONE FLOOR

MEAL FLOOR

WORKING WINDMILL

Up to c. 1900

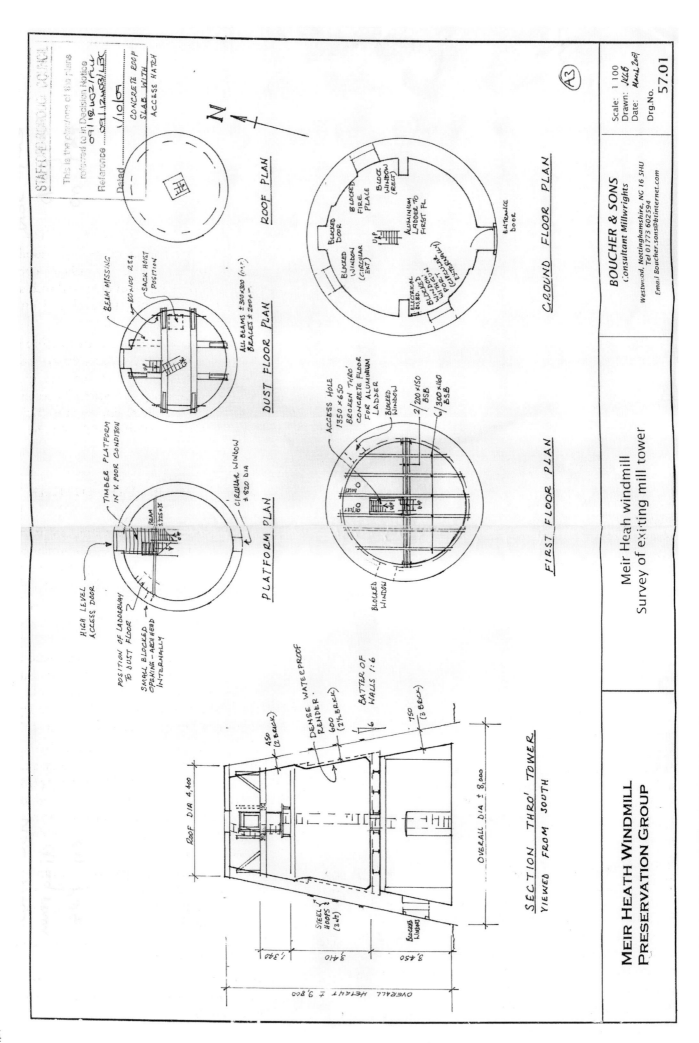

ROOF PLAN

GROUND FLOOR PLAN

DUST FLOOR PLAN

PLATFORM PLAN

FIRST FLOOR PLAN

SECTION THRO' TOWER
VIEWED FROM SOUTH

BOUCHER & SONS
Consultant Millwrights
Westwood, Nottinghamshire, NG 16 5HU
Tel 01773 602594
Email Boucher.sons@btinternet.com

Scale: 1 100
Drawn: JMcB
Date: March 2011
Drg.No.
57.01

Meir Heah windmill
Survey of exiting mill tower

**MEIR HEATH WINDMILL
PRESERVATION GROUP**

chitterie-chatterie   *A piece of bread eaten immediately after bathing.*

HERE WE ARE AGAIN

The Windmill

By Henry Wadsworth Longfellow
I look down over the farms;
In the fields of grain I see
The harvest that is to be,
And I fling to the air my arms,
For I know it is all for me.

Meir Heath Windmill Book Project

It seems the right time to start to gather a collection of interesting facts together to make a local history book. Members of Meir Heath Windmill Preservation Group have worked together to produce Behold a Giant – The Story of a Windmill.

Taking the lease from Mitchells and Butlers Company was a very big decision because once the group had that responsibility, it became necessary to be able to maintain the Grade II listed building. In order to raise money, this local history book has been published and our group is grateful for your support in buying the book.

The style is to make for an easy-reading book to just pick up and read a section which presents local history and the history of local people. As with other local history books, it is hoped it will be sold all over the world to people who have moved away from the area but who still love to read about where they grew up, as well as to local folks.

Why bother to collect all this information? Why bother to take all the photographs?

Why bother to save the very old windmill at Meir Heath?

Living in the area since 1960, I passed the windmill frequently when living at Hollies Drive, but I didn't consciously notice it. My life was one of a working person with parents to look after as well as my own family. Busy days. When I retired, I could follow my own interests and really enjoy local history and listening to what people could remember.

After writing Crown Staffordshire and Fenton in 2004, I went to Meir Heath Primary School with the local history group to talk to the children. Surprisingly, one little boy asked me why the old windmill looked such a mess; trees growing out of the bricks, aerials all over the roof and looking as if no one cared for it.

When back at home, I thought about what had been said and decided that he was right. It was a shame and someone should do something about it and save the windmill from further deterioration. It seemed sensible to form a group of people who were interested in such a project and so, in 2004, Meir Heath Windmill Group was created.

Meir Heath Windmill Group

When applying to Mitchells and Butlers Company (they are no longer a brewery) for help, it was so disheartening. They didn't want to know or to spend any money on the windmill. I tried writing to the Chief Executive of the company, to the Chairman, to the Finance Officer. Looking them all up on the internet was easy. At first no one replied to my letters.

Not easily put off, I went to see the history teacher, Simon Mottram at Meir Heath Primary School and asked him if the children could write to ask the M&B Company for help. There were 60 letters in all, beautifully written by the children and with such passion about the windmill.

My plan was subtle! On Monday I sent a letter from myself and a child's letter; Tuesday the same, Wednesday the same and so on all week. The following Monday my plan had worked because the Chairman did at last respond to the children's letters. He had a sense of humour because he put his age, 42, at the end of his letter. The children had all put their ages on their letters.

As time went on, our Committee grew. At that time I was Chairperson and I contacted various people over the next two years for help. One person who gave good advice was Gordon Hardy from Heage Windmill Group, Derbyshire. He invited us to visit and we went with Roy Deakin and had a lovely day.

John Fairbanks, the Councillor from Oulton, was very interested in the project and encouraged me to find out more about windmills. John would have loved to see it back as a working mill but the cost would be too much. It is very difficult to get funds for what we intend to do on a small scale. One morning, John arrived at Gravelly Bank with an armful of drawings of the windmill and information about how windmills' machinery worked for me to study. I was grateful to him. He had been inside the windmill and measured up to get good drawings. His enthusiasm was infectious.

Our group decided to approach the National Lottery for a grant to do the work required. A lady came to look at the windmill but said that as we didn't have the lease, they wouldn't be able to help. We were all very disappointed. It was a Catch 22 situation. If we had no money, we could do nothing and we didn't dare take a lease until we did have money.

Our group decided we needed fundraisers to start to seriously raise money. Maureen and John Upton agreed to take on the job and have been marvellous as the fundraisers for the last four years. Mary Flannagan became the Publicity Officer, Anthony Swift the Chairperson, and I became the Secretary, with Alan Mountford as Treasurer, Dorothy Bestwick as Schools Liaison Officer, and Peter Lawton, David Jones, Nigel Morley, Peter Fynn, Edna Fynn, Alfred Oakes, Roy Deakin, John Bradbeer, John Huson and Les Huson all on the Committee at that time. Even on the coldest, wettest nights, the Committee arrived at Florence Sports and Social Club once a month for the meetings.

In 2006, the group discussed the possibility of becoming a Company Limited by Guarantee in order to protect ourselves. After reading all the information, and there was a lot, and filling in copious forms, on 2 June 2006 we heard we were successful and it was a happy day.

More forms, more phone calls and more papers to fill in and on 11 August 2006 (I remember it well because on 8 August I had broken my left leg) a letter arrived to inform me that we had been granted charitable status.

The group believed that once we became a charity we would be eligible for grants.

Not long after that I received an email from a lady at Stoke Council. She sent information about a group called Grantscape Funders. We decided to ask Voluntary Action Group in Stafford to help us to fill in the forms with the correct terminology. As you all know, having an 'ology' (as Maureen Lipman used to tell us in the adverts) is a very good thing.

Steve Wilson came from Stafford to Gravelly Bank and spent two hours helping us to fill in the grant application forms. How grateful we all were for his help. The papers were sent with all the documents they asked for:

Accounts documents for the year.

Bank statements for 3 months, originals not photocopies (the Treasurer, Alan Mountford, received a phone call to ask him to find from his records the relevant documents).

Memorandum and Articles of Association to be included.

Drawings of the work to be done. Three quotations from tradesmen we invited to do the work. This involved a letter to the trader and the wait for a reply to arrange with M&B for the key to the windmill to be available. Take the trader to view. Wait for their quote to come. Rome wasn't built in a day!

Letters from the Conservation Officer to agree to work being done on a Grade II listed building.

List of all the Committee's names and occupations.

Project Plan, Business Plan, Feasibility Study and a Structural Survey (we paid a millwright of great repute, John Boucher, to do that) at a cost of £600, a special rate for us.

We needed an independent referee!

Peter Siddley, head teacher from Meir Heath Primary, came to our rescue.

Next we had to send in letters of support and that was easy because we had collected 120 excellent letters from all the people interested in the project.

Over 400 people signed a petition and 60 children from Mr Siddley's school wrote wonderful letters and did marvellous drawings of how they would like the windmill to look.

All this was parcelled up and in 2006 it cost £6.50 to post it to Grantscape Funders. Of course, then you have to wait patiently to see if you get any interest shown in your application. We heard nothing until October when an agent from Grantscape rang at 5pm on a Wednesday afternoon. He asked a few questions about the project and they were answered. He then asked who was going to be the third party in the deal. He said that our group would need to find £10,000 as our share.

Later that week, Tony and I were asked to go and visit Terry Walsh in the Radio Stoke offices. Good Times is on the radio on Sunday at lunch time. We talked about the problem getting grants and not having a solicitor to advise the group. By amazing good fortune, Ian White from Knights solicitors, Newcastle, was driving in his car and heard our plea. He stopped the car and rang Radio Stoke. Terry's assistant came into the studio where we were to give us the news that Ian would be pleased to help the group. We are very grateful to Ian White for all the help he gave. He negotiated with M&B the Heads (conditions when you take a lease) of the terms of the lease we had to have.

At the same time, we had to produce correct accounts for Companies House and were again very lucky when our supporters David and Celia Shemilt offered the services of their accountant, Robin Bagnall, who produced accounts for us.

Letters of Support

Letter from Mike Rogers to Gill Swift (February 2005)

It gives me great pleasure to write in support of your plan to restore and preserve the windmill at Meir Heath.

As a former Chief Inspector of Schools for Staffordshire, I know how important it is for pupils to have access to sites of historic interest which can be objects of study both in their own right and as focal points for the development of the basic skills of literacy and numeracy. Beyond this basic level there is much that can be done by older pupils in terms of site and position; agricultural economics; changing patterns of land use; the physics of windmills; an understanding of torque and the technical problems of construction.

The area has a surfeit of watermills, a number within easy reach, but very, very few surviving windmills. The restoration of the windmill at Meir Heath would create a teaching resource that could be allied to the watermills at Stone, and the historic parish of Caverswall with its castle, ancient church, residual open field and the adjacent enclosures to provide material for practical work and field studies by children of all ages from a wide area.

The site would have much to offer pupils from the inner-city schools in Stoke-on-Trent where later industrialisation has destroyed much of the material that would enrich the study of the stages of history covered by a learning package based on a restored windmill such as the one that could be built around the mill at Meir Heath.

May your very worthy enterprise prosper.

Letter from Mrs H R Huson, Rough Close, to Gill Swift (February 2005)

Hurrah! Someone is at long last realising the sad plight of this once wonderful structure which, if not given a new lease of life pretty soon, will be lost not only to the local community but the nation for ever.

As a former teacher at Rough Close C. of E. School, who has taken many pupils on educational walking tours around the neighbourhood, I feel very strongly that The Windmill should be preserved.

Wouldn't it be wonderful if its doors could be opened once more, so children could look inside and see how the mill looked and worked years ago in its 'heyday'? Thinking further ahead... How about turning it into a small museum! The possibilities of its use to the community are endless.

The school curriculum does include a project entitled 'How we used to live' – what better than having a working windmill on your doorstep; just relying on pictures in textbooks or gazing at a heap of bricks does nothing to inspire young minds.

Probably many newcomers to the district do not realise the part Meir Heath Windmill played in World War II. It was here that many members of the ARP were stationed. Their equipment helped to track down many aircraft.

The Windmill is steeped in history and I do care very strongly about the welfare of the Grade II listed building. I give my support to all who are committed to preserving it.

Letter from Gareth Hughes, The Society for the Protection of Ancient Buildings, to Gill Swift (15 November 2007)

Our Secretary, Simon Hudson, has passed on to me your letter of 13 November regarding the windmill.

I can confirm that the windmill had four sails for most of its working life. There is a photograph in Barry Job's book, Staffordshire Windmills, which shows the mill from the side. Although at the time only one pair of sails remained, the canister on the end of the windshaft is shown, with the mounting for the second pair of sails clearly visible. It was not unusual for mills coming to the end of their working lives to struggle on with only two sails if storm damage or decay made replacing the full set economically impossible.

Meir Heath Windmill is very interesting for several reasons and I am very pleased that restoration is being proposed (even if only of the external features). It is in an area which has no correctly restored windmills.

Most obviously, the cap and sails were turned into the wind by a tail pole. There are a few surviving examples of tail pole-winded mills elsewhere in England, but the exact arrangement in those other cases was derived from Dutch practice, with complicated diagonal bracing to give better leverage. At Meir Heath, as at several other mills in the West Midlands area, the arrangement was simpler, with only two short braces up to the rear of the cap, as shown in your photograph.

The boat-shaped cap was of a general form typical of the Midlands and North West, slightly more curved than examples further north and less so than those further south.

The sails also taper towards the tips, not only along the driving side (where the sail cloths would have been spread) but also along the relatively broad, boarded leading edge. This taper is a characteristic of windmills in Cheshire, Lancashire and North Wales, but seems to have been first suggested by the millwright William Hazeldine, who was based in Shrewsbury towards the end of the eighteenth century, whose work was admired and recorded by Thomas Telford. It would be too much to claim that Meir Heath was built by Hazeldine, but the windmill certainly shows some of the features associated with him, and is within his working area.

The circular windows are very unusual, though a few other mills had them, and it is also worth noting that the mill was clearly originally whitewashed.

In short, your project at Meir Heath represents a probably unique opportunity to recreate an important collection of features which were once typical of the windmills of the North Midlands, but which no longer survive anywhere else. It is vital that all these features are restored with absolute accuracy; otherwise the restoration will be worthless as a historical document to be understood by future generations. My tenure as Chairman of SPAB Mills Section comes to an end at the New Year and frees me to have more time available to be involved with individual mills. Meir Heath is such a worthwhile example that I would be happy to advise in any capacity as you continue to develop your plans. Please do contact me should you require any further assistance.

The Project Continued

Our Committee decided that we should have fundraising events and one of the best was the Windmill Wacky Races. Sam Plank, who had been a presenter on Radio Stoke, and his wife Verity came to a meeting and explained how to organise the event. We had a fantastic fun evening. That was in 2007 and so again in 2009 we had another Race Meeting. Sadly Sam passed away but is remembered by his many fans.

During 2008, some of the Committee went on courses at Shugborough and Gladstone Museum. These courses were 'How to make your museum family friendly' and 'How to look after artefacts'. Mary Flannagan, Gill and Tony Swift, and Dorothy Bestwick enjoyed the courses and came back with good ideas even though they didn't have a museum at that time.

It was also in 2008 that Meir Heath Primary School had a non-uniform day and raised over £200 for the Windmill Project. Also in 2008, the Secretary applied for more grants for the project. Applications were sent to the Staffordshire Environmental Fund, to Give it Sum, Grassroots and Pilgrims Trust, just to name a few.

When applications ask for a referee, Mr Peter Siddley, head teacher of Meir Heath Primary School, was always willing to help. Awards for All rang him at his school to ask for details concerning the Windmill Project and the Committee believe it is due to his help that they gave the £10,000 to do work inside the windmill.

Each application takes on average between 3 and 5 hours to prepare. Forms have to be photocopied and sometimes the postage has been £6.50 to send one application.

Maureen and John Upton arranged the Quiz Evenings, which proved to be very popular. Another event they organised was the Cream Teas and Music afternoon, enjoyed by so many senior citizens from local residential homes. The ladies and gentlemen from Eldon House, Dresden, attend many of our events along with their carers Mary Burrows and Sue. They enjoyed the Laurel and Hardy film show put on at The Crown Hotel, Longton, in the beautiful function room. Some of our other supporters are a group of lovely teenagers from Strathmore House, Dresden, who thoroughly enjoyed the show presented by Antony Mitchell-Waite, Joanne and Josh. Antony brings memorabilia and gives interesting information about Laurel and Hardy. With Joanne, Antony organises events in the Potteries for the Midnight Patrol Group. The Windmill Group are very pleased with the support that the Mitchell-Waites have given.

Early in 2009, Penny McKnight, Stafford Borough Council Senior Conservation Officer, and Martin Levie, the group's architect, met with the Chairman and Secretary to discuss planning requirements and details of work to be done inside the windmill.

During January, the group received an estimate £7,250 + VAT for E-on to dig a trench 30 metres by three-quarters of a metre deep to lay a cable for the supply of electricity to the windmill. E-on didn't send a man to the site as had been requested but worked out the estimate by using overhead aerial photography. They stated that the group would have to provide the ducting for the cable to go in and to 'reinstate' the hole with tarmac. Possible charges for tar would be another £2,000.

This came as a shock to the group when it was clear that a cable from the public house stretched to the windmill. The Secretary once again contacted E-on by email and asked for a site visit. Eventually, in March, after three more emails to different people and sending ten photographs of the boxes and cables, a man did come to see the cable and boxes. He came in a car to our surprise and didn't have a ladder so couldn't reach the box.

He said that he would come back again and so we waited another week, when he then asked to meet him and another worker on site. This time the Chairman went alone. On reaching the windmill, the Chairman was surprised to see a four-by-four vehicle. Again, no sign of a ladder. Another week went by with no news of their decision.

The solicitor was waiting to hear when to contact Mitchells & Butlers about the lease, but could not until the problem of the electricity was sorted out.

Meanwhile, the Community Fund Stoke-on-Trent Secretary, who promised £5,000 towards the boat cap, rang to say that because we hadn't raised the rest (another £25,000) we couldn't have the money promised. We were supposed to spend the money before March. We would have to see if we could get the £5,000 after April, the new financial year.

The Committee decided to engage Mr John Boucher, Millwright, to produce a structural survey. Here is a section of that report done by Mr Boucher.

Report on the Structural Condition of Meir Heath Windmill, Staffordshire

Preamble

I visited Meir Heath on 22 February 2007 at the request of the Meir Heath Windmill Preservation Group to inspect the remains of the windmill. I undertook a visual inspection of the structure, including working from ladders on the inside, but did not make any intrusive investigations. Nevertheless, I gained a good idea of the condition of the mill and do not consider any further investigations, which would have to be at considerable cost, are necessary at this stage.

Background

Meir Heath Windmill was built around 1775, and was a typical Staffordshire tower mill, comprising a substantial brick tower with internal timber floors supporting the flour-milling machinery. The tower was roofed by a rotating cap, which also supported the windmill sails, and could be rotated manually to face into the wind.

The mill operated until about 1896, when milling ceased. In 1908 it was purchased by the Staffordshire Potteries Water Company and converted into a water tower, and remained so until 1928. It was then disused until the outbreak of the Second World War, when it was taken over by the Home Guard and used as a watch tower. After the war, it was fitted with a light radio mast and served for a time as a communications centre, but has now been disused for some years.

These three main stages in the life of the mill are shown diagrammatically in Plate 4 (drawing 57/02). It is necessary to consider the differing requirements of each of these stages to follow the development of the structure, and explain the rather strange structure that exists today. When originally constructed, the mill had a conical brick tower approximately 8 metres diameter at the base and 9.6 metres high above ground, surmounted by a circular timber curb on which the cap sat. The cap was free to rotate on the curb, but whether by means of rollers or on slides is not now possible to tell. The cap had a height of about 3 metres above curb level, and carried the 'windshaft' or main axle which projected out to the front and carried the four sails.

The cap was pushed round manually so that the sails faced the wind by means of a long 'tail pole' fixed to the rear and reaching out at an angle of about 45 degrees down to ground level.

The tower had two doors on opposite sides at ground level, and windows to each floor which were originally rectangular, apart from two smaller windows near the top which appear to have always been circular. At some time prior to 1900, the two west-side windows at ground level were converted to circular, reason not known but presumably for architectural effect. Several of the windows were later blocked up in brickwork, for various reasons. From the proportions of the mill and the deduced levels of the floors, it is clear that there were originally three internal floors above the ground floor, and that the mill machinery was of the 'under driven' type.

When the mill was converted to a water tower, the two lower floors were removed, as shown in the central diagram in Plate 4. The first floor was replaced by a steel beam grillage with infill concrete, the steel beams being protected from corrosion by a coating of tar. The new first floor and walls up to above second-floor level were rendered with a thick waterproof cementitious render to form the storage tank, which is still in place. A new external doorway was inserted on the north side above second-floor level to provide access to the top of the tank, in place of one of the circular windows. At the same time, the windows at first-floor level were removed and infilled with brickwork, and the brick walls were reinforced externally with three substantial steel hoops in order to resist the outward thrust of water contained in the tank. At this stage, all traces of the original first and second floors disappeared, but the beams for the third floor (and probably boarding) were retained to provide high-level access across the tank. The cap was retained as the roof to the tank.

When the mill became a Home Guard observation point, the remains of the cap were removed and replaced by a concrete slab, having an access hole in the centre and a small shelter on top, as shown in the right-hand diagram in Plate 4. The first-floor slab was broken out locally between two of the steel beams to provided internal access, and two aluminium ships' ladders installed up to the level of the high-level external access door. Above this, a timber platform and timber stairway provided final access on to the roof. The remaining ground floor windows were filled with brickwork, one being provided with a gun port. Electric lighting may have been installed at this time.

Internally – Ground floor

The room at ground floor level had been plastered on walls and ceiling, but the plaster on the walls had deteriorated badly, and will have either to be removed completely or be re-plastered. The two doorways and the former window openings incorporate round brick arises, and there are two projecting chimney breasts on opposite sides of the mill, also with rounded arises.

There was a certain amount of surface damp on the walls; some might have penetrated through the walls, but much appears to be condensation on the fairly hard plaster rendering. The ground floor had at some time been concreted, and a polythene damp proof membrane installed.

The remains of an old electric lighting and telephone system were fixed to the walls.

From the ground floor, an aluminium 'ship's ladder' gave access to the first floor. This had clearly been installed after the water tank ceased to function, and the first floor had been broken out between two of the steel beams close to the centre of the room.

The main beams are of roughly 12" x 12" cross section, and retain the original pockets for the floor joists, and at one point, a small timber ledger which indicates the position of the original sack hoist. However, they are in poor condition, having rotten badly at the ends where originally built into the walls, where they suffered from water penetration.

Externally

There are three very prominent steel hoops constructed from steel flat bars with forged curled ends linked together with steel rings, and tensioned with a single bolted connection to each hoop. They clearly date from the time the water tank was constructed, and were installed to counteract the outward thrust of the water pressure. However, they are now quite loose against the wall and serve no structural purpose. They are in very poor condition, badly corroded, and have lost much of their original thickness, particularly at the hooked ends.

Traditionally windmills did not have gutters and downpipes as it was not possible to connect them to a rotating cap, but where caps are fixed, or new roofs constructed as in this case, proper gutters are essential to protect the walls.

The brickwork is of considerable thickness, being three bricks thick at the bottom reducing to two bricks thick at the top. This is above average thickness for windmill towers of this height, so there is no concern about residual strength.

Strength of Internal Floor

Considerable thought was given to assessing the residual strength of the internal floor. The floor comprised a spine beam of twin rolled 1904 British Standard steel beams (BSBs) of size 8" x 6", across which are laid BSBs of size 12" x 6.3" at 800 mm centres approximately, all surrounded by concrete. The beams appear to date from the construction of the water tank in 1908 and are consistent with British Standard Specification 4, first published in 1904.

The maximum depth of water in the tank was about 2.5 metres, giving a capacity of about 12,000 galls, and a static live load on the floor of about 55 tons. Analysis of the steel beam grillage showed that it was designed to take this loading.

It was not possible during the inspection to get onto the top of the flat concrete roof, but even had I been able to, little could have been learned without damaging the recently renewed weatherproof membrane. The roof slab appeared to be in reasonable condition and adequate for its present purpose. It is also performing a useful structural function in tying the top edge of the brick wall and holding it in its correct circular shape. If in the future it is desired to construct a static mill cap this could be built on top, without disturbing the slab. If however it was desired to construct a rotating cap, to restore the mill to working order, the slab would most likely have to be removed or cut back to enable a new mill curb to be constructed for the cap to turn on.

puðing time *The time to begin dinner, the first dish served.*

STARTING WORK

The Windmill

By Henry Wadsworth Longfellow
I hear the sound of flails
Far off, from the threshing-floors
In barns, with their open doors,
And the wind, the wind in my sails,
Louder and louder roars.

The shot blaster – Mr A Shaw Commercial Services

**The Two Scaffolders Andrew Wood, Damian Northcup and Gill Swift
The Project Manager**

**Metal Bands on the mill
when it was a water tower**

31

New beam put in to top floor
(By kind permission of A Swift)

Boat cap (cedar wood)

Hodson Builders – Leon Bailey, Phil Hancock and Mick Alcock

Sub-committee – M Levie, M Flannagan, P Hancock, P Lawton, B Morris and J Bradbeer

Workers passing cap sections to top of mill

There was no electricity in the windmill so the workmen tried to make tea using a portable gas stove – the Chairman took up flasks of soup to the men

Feeding in beams – P Hancock and J Hegerty
(Photos by A Swift)

Phil Hancock (the Builder) and Lizzie Meek from Radio Stoke

Project Manager G Swift

N Clowes and L Bailey passing bricks

Scaffolder with Chairman A Swift
(Photo D L Swift)

Evening Sentinel Article

Restoration grant will be lost without money

GRANT FIGHT: Meir Heath Windmill Action Group members with secretary Gill Swift, second right, outside the landmark.

£10,000 by Monday or bust

By Iain Robinson

CAMPAIGNERS behind a £100,000 project to restore an historic windmill have until Monday to secure a promise of £10,795 funding.

Meir Heath Windmill Action Group needs to find the money within 3 days after asking for £95,000 grant funding to cover the cost of renovating the 1775 Grade II listed windmill in Hilderstone Road.

The group, which has worked on the project for four years and raised funds, applied for the cash because it wants to take over the lease for the dilapidated landmark from current owner M&B Brewery

But the group has now been told its bid to Grantscape will be rejected unless £10,795 third-party funding can be found by Monday.

Secretary Gill Swift says the group had been unaware of the need for third-party funding.

She said: "We had sent off the documents Grantscape asked for, and thought things sounded quite promising. Then I had a phone call from them asking who will be contributing the £10,795 third-party donation that is required. It would be a terrible shame if we lost out because we couldn't get £10,000."

(By kind permission of the Sentinel Newspaper)

New hatch and ladder

Beams inserted into top of windmill

Ribs Added to Boat cap

Surprise Phone Call

Gill's husband, Anthony, who is the group's Chairman, said: *"It is a chicken and egg situation. We can't get the lease without the grant money, but they won't give us the grant until we get the lease. The only way around it is to get a firm promise of funding from a third party. M and B has offered us a lease for a peppercorn rent."*

What to do? I rang Councillor Shaw at Meir Heath.

Councillor Barry Shaw listened to me and said he would think about it and make a list of funders he knew. As sure as his word he did and later that night a list was pushed through my letterbox. I was grateful for his help.

I rang one or two other people and the Sentinel and at 8.00pm had a chat to a reporter who said he would put an appeal in the paper on Saturday and he did.

Saturday was the day we had counted the money from the dance which had taken place on the Friday. The Chairman took it to the Treasurer's house, who at that time was Mr Alan Mountford. The Secretary had just received the Evening Sentinel and read the article seen here. Iain Robinson kept his promise and a good photo and information in the Sentinel appeared as promised.

The Secretary was reading the paper when Janet from Target Window Company rang to say that her company would donate £500 to help. What a wonderful offer and the money, when received, was spent wisely on the windmill.

The second call was rather a puzzle. The Secretary didn't know what to think. A gentleman rang but wouldn't give his name. He said that as a boy he had played in the windmill and would like to help. At that point the Secretary wondered if it was a hoax call but continued to listen.

His next question surprised her.

"Do you believe in God, Mrs Swift?"

The Secretary replied cautiously, *"Yes I do".*

The caller then said, *"Why do you believe in God?"*

The Secretary said that she had a new granddaughter who had been born prematurely. Many friends and family had prayed for the baby and the little girl, Olivia, had survived. Born weighing 1 pound 5 ounces, she was now 6 months old.

The caller then said, *"That is good. I believe in God who has been good to me. I will give your group the £10,000 you need. Is that ladder still in the mill?"*

The Secretary said to the caller, *"Yes it is. You can come and see it if you wish,"* still thinking this was all a hoax.

The caller next said, *"You think this is a hoax call, don't you? I am a Christian and like to help people. Ring up my solicitor on Monday and he will arrange it all for you."*

The Secretary thanked the caller, saying she looked forward to Monday.

The caller's next words were, *"Mrs Swift, enjoy your weekend. I'm glad you believe in God."*

The Chairman came back at that point as the Secretary put the phone down.

Explaining the call and discussing it, they both decided not to tell the Committee because it must be a hoax. Monday came and, as usual about 9.00am, the couple were having breakfast when the phone rang.

"Hello, it's me, John. I've rung my solicitor, and he is waiting for your call. Here is the phone number." The Secretary started to believe this was not a hoax. She rang the number and the solicitors' secretary answered and put the call through to the solicitor who said he would arrange it all.

We just needed someone to promise to pay it so the grant application could go through. We either needed a single large donor or several smaller ones, and for larger donations we could look at providing memorial plaques for loved ones inside the finished windmill.

Letter from Solicitors to Gill Swift (2 November 2007)

Many thanks for your letter of the 18 October received during my absence on holiday. I have spoken to my client, who is quite happy, as you are aware, to support the group to the extent of £10,000. His intention is, of course, to guarantee that sum to assist you in securing the necessary grant aid.

Sadly the group didn't get the grant from Grantscape. They had so many applications and were sorry not to help our group.

Letter from M&B to Chairman A Swift (30 January 2008)

I refer you to my letter dated 22 March 2006 addressed to Mrs G Swift. In this letter I made it very clear that "M&B does not wish to fund or lead a project to restore the mill or to carry out any of the activities associated with the mill that you suggest". I also made it clear that M and B "will of course continue to meet our legal obligations in respect of the windmill and follow all legitimate directions from Staffordshire Borough Council (SSC)". The situation has not changed, nor is it likely to change.

Work at the Windmill

Week One (30 November 2009)

At last we are going to start work at the windmill!

It is the 30 November 2009 and Tony and I went to the windmill as Phil Hancock and two of his workmen were setting up a fence around the site. They also had a Portaloo inside the fence because it was not possible to use the pub toilets.

I asked Adam, the public house manager, where the electricians were. Our group had been told by the representative of M&B that the electricity supply would be fixed by this date. It wasn't! Adam said that he expected them today but they had not arrived. When we went home, the first thing that I did was to email the M&B representative to ask what had happened to cause the delay. The time was 1.00pm.

At 6.00pm there still was no reply. Trying to be patient, it was upsetting to go the next day to the windmill and find that Phil the builder and his men were finding it difficult without lights and power. Checking the email at home, M&B had replied stating that electricity could not be fixed until the lease was signed. This was a puzzle because I signed the lease with John Bradbeer twice; once on 23 October 2009 and again on 5 November 2009, because M&B solicitors stated that there was a typographical error in the first one. Later, when a copy of the lease arrived, it had been signed on 23 August 2009 by M&B officials. Why did they wait so long before allowing us to sign? The builder was having a struggle with no electric, and so fetched a generator at a cost of £130 plus VAT a week. This was a real problem and so another email went to M&B, explaining that our group would be charging them for the generator. A message came back stating that the electric would be done by Thursday, Friday at the latest.

Phil and his men have had to make it safe to work inside the mill and have put acros in to hold up ceilings on all floors. He wishes to meet the architect on Friday noon to decide the best action to take regarding the beams because, now he has a light, he can see how dangerous they really are. I rang the Stafford Borough Conservation Officer to see if she would come on Friday to check the water on the walls inside. Phil believes that the bricks will be spoilt if we remove the plaster. Today I spoke to Adam, the public house manager, to see if the builder could use the water supply at the Inn. Adam was very helpful and agreed. The weather was awful and Tony took up a flask of soup for the workmen. One of the men, Mick, had a tiny stove with gas ring and was making tea. In spite of such terrible working conditions, the workmen were very cheerful. Later that day the scaffolding arrived. It was the Atlas Company. We took photographs of it being unloaded. Phil took photographs at the top of the mill inside for the records. Phil explained that he wants the site to be kept tidy at all times.

Each time we visited the windmill, we wore the hard hats we bought last week. Mine is red and Tony's a yellow colour. We have bought Olivia, our granddaughter, a 'Bob the Builder' yellow hat and she loves it.

3 December 2009 – Tony went to the Mill at 2.30pm. The workers had been busy and Phil showed Tony the rotten beams which had been removed from the inside top mill. Lying on the grass, the beams were really a mess. About 5 feet long and 9 inches thick. Phil was pleased with how well work was going, in spite of no electricity. Today his men made staging at the top level so they had a platform to work on. The round window at the top has been taken out and also the door.

During his visit, Tony went to see if the electricians had fixed the electric sub-meter under the stairs in the public house. The men arrived and said the work on the meter would be done by Friday, 4 December 2009, and the electricians worked all day to fix the supply; this to cost us £1,150.

The architect came as promised at noon and with Tony and Phil the builder discussed the beams. The builder thought that it would be an extra £2,000 approx. to make the beams safe. Again this would involve hire of a crane at £350 for half a day, £2,000 for the oak and the rest for labour to make holes in the tower to feed in the beams and then make good the brickwork on the two holes. At present, the quotation for the job from the builder did not include the cost of this section of work.

The Chairman (Tony) told the builder to prop up the roof with acros for the time being until we could see if there was enough money to do the job. Tony came home and fetched soup for the three workmen because it was bitterly cold again. At 3.30 pm the same day, I went up to see if the electrics were finished. They weren't. Two men were still working and they promised me that it would be done by 5.00pm. This was the end of a busy Week One. I passed the notebook to Mr John Bradbeer, one of the group's directors, and this is what happened the week he kept the work log.

Week Two – John Bradbeer Reports

Monday 7 December 2009 – Today I visited the Windmill at 2.15pm and met Mick and his partner working on descaling the lower walls inside. They showed me the rotten timbers brought down from the top floor. It was very cold inside with poor working conditions. It was cold, dismal and wet. One of the builder's men, Mick, said that it really needed a lot of ventilation to try and dry out the walls. I noticed that the site was safe with fencing around the area and that a skip had arrived and was inside the fencing. Tomorrow the builder expects the shot blaster to arrive early to do the work on the lintels on the ground floor. I was told that Mr Hancock and the boys would be back on Wednesday.

Wednesday 9 December 2009 – The lads were hard at work when I arrived today. The shot blaster had left the site the day before and there were 3 to 4 inches of dust and sand all over the floor and walls. The men started the clean-up operation and it was being bagged for the skip. Feeling brave, I went up to the very top of the windmill and saw where the beams had been taken out and where work was to be done bricking up round the doors and windows on Thursday. A heater was on to try and dry out the walls and I was impressed by a great set of lads working so hard in such cold conditions.

Friday 11 December 2009 – Phil, the builder, arrived at the windmill the same time as I did and said that he was there to meet Penny McKnight.

Week Three – Dorothy Bestwick, Treasurer, Reports

Thursday 15 December 2009 – I went to the windmill at 12.30pm to chronicle the progress of the work. It was cold, damp and foggy and on the ground floor, Leon was rendering between the roof beams. The removal of the plaster from the walls highlighted the fireplace on the opposite wall on the top floor, following the removal of the old door and frame. Dennis was installing a new beam. As the brickwork had deteriorated, Dennis was proceeding with work rebuilding the bricks on the right-hand side of the doorway. It was very cold.

17 December 2009 – At 10.40 am I arrived at the Windmill to see that Leon had completed the rendering of the ceiling between the beams. He went on to remove the old plaster from the walls with hand tools. It was very difficult because it was so cold.

18 December 2009 – I made my final visit to the windmill today. Part of the wall inside had been rendered in line with the Conservation Officer's instructions. Three of Mr Hancock's workmen were applying lime wash to the ceiling and walls of the windmill. They informed me that they were to apply five coats. This was the last day they would work since the Christmas holidays were starting and they wouldn't be back until 4 January 2010.

Mrs G Swift Project Manager Reports

19 February 2010 – Snow again. Bitterly cold. No work can be done. Terribly sorry for the workmen. The cedar cladding should arrive today. Inside not as wet as previously. Lime wash is drying slowly. I asked Phil, the builder, for information concerning heaters.

8 March – Phil Hancock sent in quote for the following work:

Erect a scaffold, supply generator, transport water, fence off working area, install welfare facilities, rake out area of cement and sand mortar, remove shaled brickwork, remove foliage, apply 2 8 mm coats of lime render with one 6 mm top coat, apply sealer to new render, cover with two coats of paint, remove all spoil from site.

10 March – 9.00am Gill and Tony arrived at the windmill. A huge crane had already been set up. Legs were extended from the base of the lorry. Protective iron plates put down on the tarmac.

Ibstock Cory Ask for Information

As part of the agreement for the grant from Ibstock Cory Trust, the Secretary/Project manager had to send a report of work to Sarah Myers, Ibstock Cory's Press Officer. This had to be done on a number of occasions as requested.

Email to Ibstock Cory Trust asked for by Sarah Myers the Press Officer - Report of Work Done at Meir Heath Windmill Project, 2 March 2010

Today the boat-cap roof is finished and the sub-committee, architect and builder all met to view the boat cap. The cedar wood is fixed onto the frame as designed by Martin Levie, the architect. The extreme cold weather had made it difficult for the builder and his team. Work stopped last week because it was too dangerous for the men to climb. Frost on the boards made work impossible. However, with some extra scaffolding fixed to give extra height, the work began again. The end door was put into place and the boat cap finished. Enclosed are photographs of the very strong frame fixed first which supports the cedar cladding. Today, while the weather is better, the builder has three men taking damaged bricks out of the tower walls and replacing them with the best-match second-hand bricks the Chairman obtained locally. The building sub-committee met and spoke to a technical adviser for lime render, the details to be sent to Penny McKnight for her approval. The Secretary is to get quotations for the work of rendering the outside of the tower. I hope that this report meets with your approval.

Yours sincerely, Gill Swift

Congratulations – Celebrating Phase 1 of the Windmill Project

The Committee decided that we should have a celebration party and invite everyone who had helped with the project. It was 10 June 2010 and held at the Windmill Inn. Councillor Millichap, the Mayor of Stafford, and his wife, the Mayoress Mrs Millichap, agreed to join us along with the Deputy Mayor of Stone, Councillor Green, and his Deputy Mayoress, Mrs Green.

Our other guests were Angela Haymonds, the Trust Secretary representing Ibstock Cory Trust, Keith Williams, representing Staffordshire Environmental Trust, Mrs Brayford from Fulford Parish Council, Terry Walsh, Chairman of the Community Foundation Grassroots, Martin Levie the architect, Phil Hancock our builder and all our Directors and Committee members. Apologies were sent from the representative of Awards for All who could not attend, and from Councillor Ian Parry of Stafford County Council.

The Secretary, Gill Swift, explained to the visitors how the project had been completed so far and thanked all for their interest and support.

The two singing dolls were shown and sang 'Forever Friends'. The dolls are taken by the Chairman and Secretary to meetings when they talk about the Windmill Project so that the children remember the Windmill Project. A certificate is also given to the group. A bit of humour goes a long way.

A certificate and a poster of the painting of the Windmill done by Roy Deakin was given to the guests, who all showed their delight at receiving the gifts. A buffet was then available and the guests enjoyed the food and the wonderful cake, which had been made and presented by Andrea and Gerald Bagnall. The windmill model on the cake, when wound up, had sails that moved and caused much interest.

After the food was served, the guests enjoyed songs sung by the group from the U3A (University of the Third Age) at Stone, The Stoneagers, conducted by Pam Sinclair. To end the proceedings, the Chairman, Anthony Swift, thanked the singers and all the visitors for joining the celebrations.

The Census Records from 1841 to 1891

CENSUS 1841			
George Walker	*(40)*	• *Miller & Baker*	
Ann	*(40)*	• *Wife*	

CENSUS 1851			
George Walker	*(52)*	• *Baker & Flour Dealer*	Burslem
Ann	*(51)*	• *Wife*	Hanley
George	*(14)*	• *Nephew Apprentice*	Hanley?

CENSUS 1871			
John Hall	*(68)*	• *Miller*	Gentleshaw
Ann	*(63)*	• *Wife*	Stone
William	*(28)*	• *Son Miller*	Cannock

CENSUS 1881			
John Hall	*(78)*	• *Retired Miller*	Living at Rough Close
Ann	*(73)*	• *Wife*	Living at Rough Close
Emily	*(46)*	• *Daughter-in-Law*	Living at Rough Close
William Hall	*(38)*		Living at Seedy Mill, Curborough, Staffs
Eliza	*(38)*	• *Wife*	Living at Seedy Mill, Curborough, Staffs
Florence	*(7)*	• *Daughter*	Living at Seedy Mill, Curborough, Staffs
"Dusty Miller Beer House"			
George Walker	*(42)*	• *Miller*	Born Leek, Staffs.
Edwin G	*(21)*	• *Son* • *Innkeeper*	Stone.

CENSUS 1891			
"Dusty Miller"			
Thomas Prince	*(60)*	• *Miller*	Born Ipstones
Emily	*(55)*	• *Wife*	Stone

Chris and Tom Preston Landlords of Windmill Inn (2012)

Stoneage Singers inside the Windmill Inn at the Celebration party

Richard Ash Broster

Inside the porch at the Windmill Inn is a notice about the mill. No one seems to know the author of the document and it seems to have a few anomalies in it.

At the beginning of the document it states that Richard Ash Broster was 110 (one hundred and ten) when he died. It then states:

'this claim must be looked at critically.'

Richard and Judith Creswell have sent to the group the death certificate of Richard Ash Broster, which shows he died when he was 79.

The document is as follows.

'This small brick mill was reputedly built by Richard Ash Broster who lived to the age of 110. However, as Broster was born in 1771 and the mill was in existence in 1775, this claim must be looked at critically.

The windmill is clearly shown on Yates Map of 1775 and Greenwoods 1828 map. The mill had 4 sails, boat cap, tailpole and cartwheel for luffing.

The mill worked until about 1885 when the eyesight of the miller, a Mr Prince, failed.

The tower of the mill was used as an observation post by the Home Guard during the last war. It also has a water tank fitted onto the top, used to supply domestic water before the present reservoir was constructed nearby. The tower presently forms part of the Bass Charrington radio communications system.

Records regarding The Windmill as a public house are almost non-existent although in 1847 the miller, a Mr Thomas Shredder, had a beer house and it is probable that the original building was the miller's house.

The earliest reference to The Windmill as a public house was in 1851 when the victualler was a Mr John Shelley

Let's get the facts correct.

There is some information concerning this gentleman where he is given the age 110. It must be a typing error. Richard and Judy Cresswell have sent me the details and correct date as seen on the death certificate. Richard Ash Broster died 2 February 1890 at Blythe Marsh, Dilhorne, age 79 years (Corn Miller).

There is a birth certificate dated 16 July 1846 for Thomas; son of Richard Ash Broster (Miller). Judy sent the following information. Richard Ash Broster's daughter, Henrietta Constance, married Reginald Douglas Cresswell, who was Richard's grandfather. Blythe mill was owned by the Brosters until 1921.

Judith visited two graves at St Nicholas Church, Fulford. The inscription on one was 'To the memory of Frances, the wife of Thomas Broster of Blythe Marsh Mill and daughter of Richard and Mary Ash, who died 8 June 1861, age 86 years'. The second was 'To the memory of Mary, the wife of Richard Ash, late of the Windmill, who departed this life in August 1820 in the 70th year of her life'.

LOT 3.

A FIELD of good OLD TURF LAND, containing 2A. 0R. 25P., called Wood Field situate on the same side of the Road and within a short distance of Lot 1, bounded by the Black Wood and Lands of the Duke of Sutherland, and in the occupation of Mr. Heapy.

LOT 4.

An excellent FIELD of PASTURE LAND, containing 1A. 3R. 26P., situate on the opposite side of the Road to and directly in front of the Black Wood, on the Mear Heath and Hilderstone Road, close to the last Lot, bounded by Lands of Sir Lionel Pilkington, Bart. and Mrs. Ash, and in the occupation of Mr. Heapy.

NORMACOT TOWNSHIP.

LOT 5.

A valuable and eligible FIELD of BUILDING LAND, containing 5A. 0R. 10P., called Rabbit Field, situate at Shooter's Hill, on the right of the Road leading from Mear Heath to Windmill Hill, and within a short distance of Mear Heath, commanding most extensive views of the surrounding country, bounded by Lands of the Duke of Sutherland, Mrs. Bailey and [...]

Registration District   Cheadle

1846.   Birth in the Sub-district of   Dilhorne   in the   County of Stafford

No.	When and where born	Name, if any	Sex	Name, and surname of father	Name, surname and maiden surname of mother	Occupation of father	Signature, description and residence of informant	When registered	Signature of registrar
	Sixteenth July 1846 Blythe Marsh Dilhorne	Thomas	Boy	Richard Ash Broster	Mary Broster formerly Finney	Miller	Mary Broster Mother Blythe Marsh	Ninth August 1846	Jonathan Whalley Registrar.

Certified to be a true copy of an entry in a register in my custody.

TION—It is an offence to falsify a certificate or to make or knowingly use a false certificate or a copy of a false certificate intending it to be accepted as genuine to the prejudice of any person, or to possess a certificate knowing it to be false without lawful authority.

J M Taylor   Superin

6th Januar

CERTIFIED COPY of an   ENTRY OF DEATH
Pursuant to the Births and   Deaths Registration Act 1953

Registration District   Cheadle

1890   Death in the Sub-district of   Dilhorne   in the   County of Stafford

No.	When and where died	Name and surname	Sex	Age	Occupation	Cause of death	Signature, description, and residence of informant	When registered
226	Second February 1890 Blythmarsh Dilhorne R.S.D	Richard Ash Broster	Male	79 years	Corn Miller	Senile Decay Congestion of Lungs Certified by J.W.Dawes M B	Emma Stanyer Daughter present at the death Park Crossing Caverswall	Fourth February 1890

Certified to be a true copy of an entry in a register in my custody.

CAUTION—It is an offence to falsify or to alter or to make or knowingly use a false certificate or a copy of a false certificate intending it to be accepted as genuine to the prejudice of any person, or to possess a certificate knowing it to be false without lawful authority.

J M Taylor   Superint

6th January

Conditions therein contained. The said sum of £1,000 shall on completion be paid out of the amount of the Purchase-money, hereby agreed to be given for the entirety; and if the Purchaser cannot complete the said Contract or his Contract as to the Five-sixths, he shall be at liberty to give up his entire purchase, on exercising the said power in favour of the Vendors.

LOT 17.

A COMPACT AND MOST

VALUABLE FREEHOLD FARM

Situate at *MODDERSHALL, near STONE,*

Comprising a good and substantial FARM HOUSE, containing Kitchen, Parlour, Back Kitchen, Three Chambers and Two Attics, Scullery, Cellar and Dairy, with good Homestead of Cart Hovel for Four Carts, Open Shed for Four Carts, Stable for Six Horses, and Loft over, Cowhouse with Barn over, Hackney Stable for Two Horses with Loft over, and a small Gig House and Gardens; also a

FLINT MILL, called MODDERSHALL MILL,

In good working order, with Two Water Wheels of 18 feet diameter, on one Wheel a Pan of 12 feet diameter, Two Arcs, Wash-tub, Two Ovens, Drying Kiln, and on the other Wheel a Pan of 8 feet diameter.

Also a good new COTTAGE, in No 53, with Cowshed and Yard, and Twenty-three Pieces of ARABLE, MEADOW, and PASTURE LAND, adjoining together most conveniently for occupation, and lying within a Ring Fence, and containing altogether 71A. 0R. 20P., more particularly described in the following Schedule,

And PEW No. 41 on the Ground Floor of STONE CHURCH.

No. on Plan.	Description.	Cultivation.	A.	R.	P.
44	Little Wood	Arable	3	2	28
45	Ware Field	Pasture	6	0	37
46	Bear Hole	Ditto	0	1	8
47	Pool Field and Rough	Arable	4	3	34
48	Bear Holes and Far Meadow	Meadow	5	0	34
49	Little Horse Pasture	Arable	3	1	30
50	Lime Field	Pasture	2	0	37
51	Thistley Fields	Arable	5	2	37
52	Middle Meadow	Meadow	3	0	6
53	Barn Meadow	Ditto	3	1	30
54	Barn and Rickyard		0	0	30
55	Garden	Pasture	0	3	20
57	Whey Meadow	Ditto	3	1	3
58	Little Meadow	Ditto	0	1	22
59	Homestead, Yard, and Garden		0	1	1
60	Mill		0	1	5
61	Mill Croft	Pasture	0	1	0
62	Orchard	Ditto	0	1	8
63	Road	Road	0	1	6
64	Mill Hill	Arable	4	3	26
65	Mill Meadow	Meadow	3	1	22
66	Garden	Garden	0	0	31
67	Roadway, &c.	Road	0	0	24
68	New Pasture Field	Pasture	3	0	0
69	Little Meadow	„	2	1	13
70	Lower Pasture Field (Sidmouth)	„	1	3	13
71	Little Meadow near Wood	„	1	1	8
72	Far Pasture Field	„	3	0	0
73	Upper Hob Hay	Arable	1	3	39
74	Lower Hob Hay	„	2	1	35
75	Hob Hay Wood	Wood	2	0	33
			A. 71	0	20

STAFFORDSHIRE.

PLANS AND PARTICULARS

OF VALUABLE

FREEHOLD PUBLIC-HOUSE,

BUILDING, ACCOMMODATION AND OTHER LANDS,

SITUATE NEAR MEAR HEATH, LONGTON, AND STONE.

TO BE SOLD BY AUCTION,

BY

MR. HENRY GILLARD,

ON TUESDAY, THE 18th OF MARCH, 1879,

AT FOUR FOR FIVE O'CLOCK IN THE AFTERNOON PUNCTUALLY.

SUBJECT TO CONDITIONS, THE FOLLOWING

PROPERTIES,

SITUATE

IN THE TOWNSHIPS OF STALLINGTON, NORMACOT, KIBBLESTONE, AND FULFORD.

The Tenants of all the Lots (except 8 and 9) are under Notice to Quit at Lady-day.

To anyone requiring Accommodation Land, sites for Building purposes, or a sound and profitable Investment, the above presents a good opportunity.

If required, a fair amount of the Purchase-money of each Lot may remain on Mortgage.

Plans and Particulars, and any information, may be obtained from the AUCTIONEER, Stafford; Mr. MINOR, Land Agent, Stoke Park, Market Drayton; Mr. GINDERS, Land Agent, The Hough, Stafford; or Messrs HAND, BLAKISTON, EVERETT & HAND, Solicitors, Stafford.

R & W. WRIGHT, PRINTERS, STAFFORD.

A FIELD of PASTURE LAND, called Gravelly Moss, containing 5A. 0R. 35P., situate at Moss Gate, in the Township of Fulford, within a short distance of Stallington, Hilderstone and Stone, bounded by the Brooms Farm, Lands of William Simkin, Esq., Mr. Shardlow and Mr. Love, and occupied by Mr. Heapy.

TOWNSHIP OF KIBBLESTONE.
Lot 7.

All those FIVE COTTAGES and GARDEN, situate at Stonefield, near Stone, adjoining the Road from Stone to Longton, and occupied by John Wood, William Latham and others.

Lot 8.

A valuable FIELD of good OLD TURF LAND, containing 4A. 3R. 5P., situate at Stonefield aforesaid, occupied by Mr. John Stansfield, and bounded by Barlaston Glebe Land and the Turnpike Road leading from Stone to Longton and the Road to Meaford.

This Lot is admirably situate for the erection of a House.

Lot 9.

A NEWLY-ERECTED MESSUAGE, with substantial and well-built Cowsheds, Piggeries, and excellently-arranged Out-buildings; also THREE FIELDS of superior MEADOW and PASTURE LAND, containing 10A. 1R. 29P., all adjoining and in a ring fence, situate at Stonefield, within a short distance of Stone, and abutting up to the Road leading from Stone to Longton.

This Lot is in the occupation of Mr. John Stansfield, and is bounded by Lands of J. F. Wileman, Esq., J. Done, Esq., and Mr. Blakeman, and lies within a short distance of the Residences of Mrs. Armitage

TOWNSHIP OF STALLINGTON.
Lot 1.

The valuable Old-established and FULL-LICENSED PUBLIC-HOUSE and PREMISES, called the Windmill Inn, situate at Windmill Hill, near Mear Heath, in the County of Stafford, now occupied by Mr. Heapy.

This Lot adjoins the Turnpike Road leading from Mear Heath to Hilderstone and Sandon, is close to the Junction of the Four Road Ends from Blythe Bridge, Stone, Hilderstone, and Mear Heath, within three miles of Longton and two of Blythe Bridge, and admirably situated for doing a good business.

TOWNSHIP OF KIBBLESTONE.
Lot 2.

A valuable piece of MEADOW LAND, called Rushton's Field, containing 4A. 2R. 7P., with the Garden or Stackyard adjoining, containing 17P., occupied by Mr. Heapy; also the TOLLHOUSE and GARDEN adjoining, occupied by Mr. Marsh.

This Lot, which is situate nearly opposite Lot 1, is surrounded by Lands of Sir Lionel Pilkington, Bart., and Mrs. Bailey, and is well adapted for Building purposes, being high and dry, and having a frontage of about 280 yards to the Turnpike Road leading from Mear Heath to Hilderstone and Sandon.

Lot 3.

A FIELD of good OLD TURF LAND, containing 2A. 0R. 25P., called Wood Field, situate on the same side of the Road and within a short distance of Lot 1, bounded by the Black Wood and Lands of the Duke of Sutherland, and in the occupation of Mr. Heapy.

Lot 4.

An excellent FIELD of PASTURE LAND, containing 1A. 3R. 26P., situate on the opposite side of the Road to and directly in front of the Black Wood, on the Mear Heath and Hilderstone Road, close to the last Lot, bounded by Lands of Sir Lionel Pilkington, Bart.

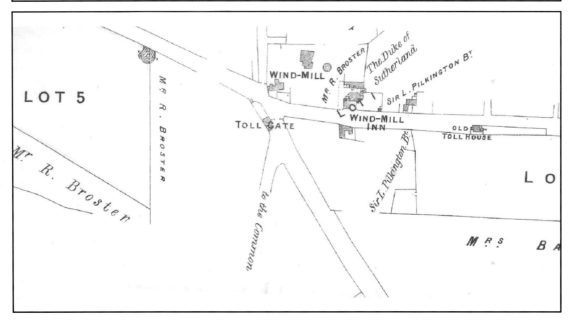

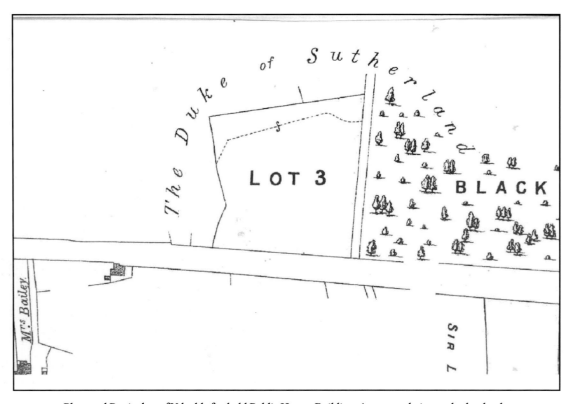

Plans and Particulars of Valuable freehold Public House, Building, Accommodation and other lands,
situated near MEAR [sic] Heath, LONGTON and STONE.

plumper

A plumper is a fine, thin, light ball that old ladies who have lost their side teeth hold in their mouths to plump out their cheeks, which else would hang like leathern bags.

THE STORY CONTINUES

People Who Helped the Project

Many of the photographs of the top of the mill were taken by the builder, Mr Phil Hancock.

Letter to Mrs G Swift from Hodson Building Services Ltd (28 July 2008)

Re: Works to the Windmill – Meir Heath

Further to your request and subsequent to our inspection of the work involved, please find our estimate for your consideration.

Internal Works – Ground floor

Remove the plaster to the walls and ceiling. Shot-blast the steel beams.

Treat the steel with fire-retardant paint. Make good the cement mortar joints to the walls. Clean down the walls. Remove the brickwork to the three window openings.

Make good the reveals. Supply and install three new timber windows & 2 beams.

Plaster out the ceiling. Apply a Lime wash finish to the walls and ceiling.

First Floor

Remove the existing hatch. Supply and install a new ladder for maintenance.

Fit a new access hatch. Remove the timber beams no longer required.

Supply and install a new fixed door and frame to include the erection of a safe working platform. All spoil to be removed from site.

External Works

Fence off the work area. Install welfare facilities. Erect a scaffold. Repair the lower steel band. Clean down the brickwork. Make good areas of damaged brickwork (5 square metres approx.). Remove all spoil from site.

Listed Buildings

Listing helps us acknowledge and understand our shared history. It marks and celebrates a building's special architectural and historic interest, and also brings it under the consideration of the planning system so that some thought will be taken about its future.

The older a building is, the more likely it is to be listed.

All buildings built before 1700 which survive in anything like their original condition are listed, as are most of those built between 1700 and 1840. The criteria become tighter with time, so that post-1945 buildings have to be exceptionally important to be listed. A building has normally to be over 30 years old to be eligible for listing.

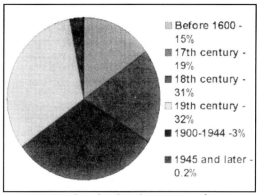

Legend:
- Before 1600 - 15%
- 17th century - 19%
- 18th century - 31%
- 19th century - 32%
- 1900-1944 - 3%
- 1945 and later - 0.2%

Pie chart detailing the age range of listed buildings in the UK

Categories of Listed Buildings

Grade I buildings are of exceptional interest, sometimes considered to be internationally important; only 2.5% of listed buildings are Grade I.

Grade II* buildings are particularly important buildings of more than special interest; 5.5% of listed buildings are Grade II*.

Grade II buildings are nationally important and of special interest; 92% of all listed buildings are in this class and it is the most likely grade of listing for a home owner.

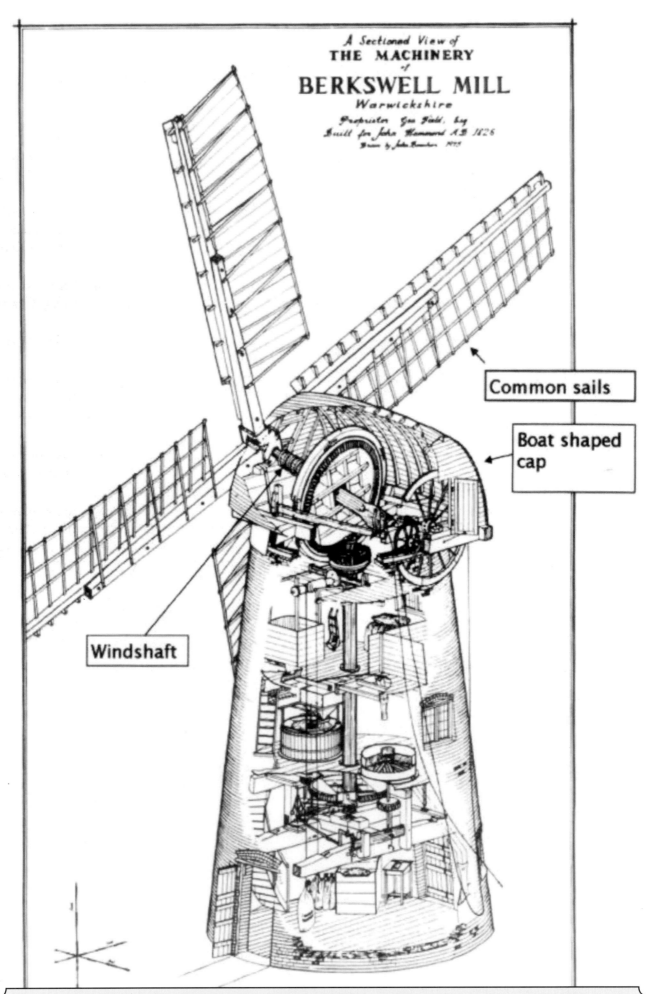

A Sectioned View of
THE MACHINERY
of
BERKSWELL MILL
Warwickshire

Common sails

Boat shaped cap

Windshaft

This mill shows the machinery set out as the windmill probably would have been at Meir Heath.
This is the work the Committee asked Mr Hancock, the builder, to do a quotation for.

Letter from Martin Levie,
Harrison Wood Architecture & Construction Consultancy

We are pleased to be involved with the Meir Heath Windmill Preservation Group in their quest to undertake repairs, refurbishment and restoration to the old Windmill building, in the grounds of The Windmill public house at Meir Heath.

For too many years, the building has been forgotten and left to decay. Thanks to the actions and attention of the Meir Heath Windmill Preservation Group, this building is now on the way to recovering its Landmark status with the initial phases of repair and refurbishment having been carried out.

From various pieces of historical information and available pictures, we have been able to design and have constructed a replacement 'boat-cap' roof – given its name due to its appearance and formation to that of a boat's hull, – and similar in appearance to that which would have previously existed, clad in cedar strip timber, providing the building with its 'head-dress' and thus providing a new imposing definition to the building.

The design process has involved extensive consultations with the Stafford Borough Council Planning Department and Conservation Officer concerning this Grade II Listed Building, through the Planning and Listed Building Consent procedures.

While all the features of the original building at this stage have not been practical, nor required to be replicated, the important essence of the former Windmill is being recovered.

The former Windmill has quite a history since coming into being as a Mill during the late 18th Century, to having construction changes for it to be used as a water tower and as a Home Guard observation post during the Second World War.

Of course, the project for renovation will need to continue here-from to ensure that the integrity of the structure will be maintained.

We offer our sincere best wishes to the Meir Heath Preservation Group in their quest and fundraising activities to ensure that this historically important building can be retained and further restoration works undertaken to maintain its position in the history of the local area.

The architectural Practice of Harrison Wood is long-established in the Longton area of Stoke-on-Trent, having been formed in 1957 by Stanley Harrison, before becoming Harrison and Wood in 1971 and further changes in the Practice in 1992.

We continue to provide a full range of architectural services and associated consultancy services for most types of building project, whether they are residential, commercial or industrial – new build or extensions or alterations.

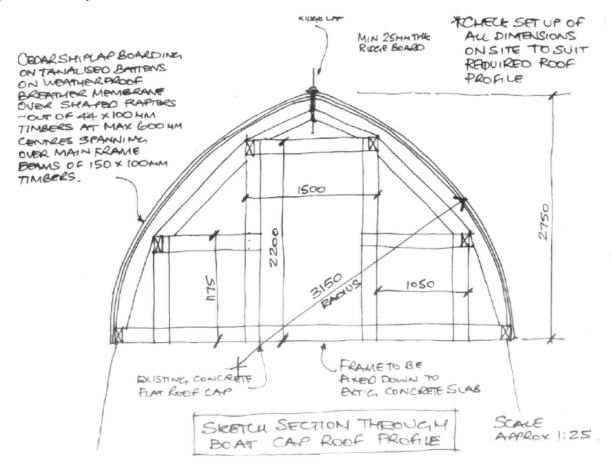

Photo of Meir Heath Windmill painting by Lawton

What a Picture, What a Photograph!

John Banks' father was Ernest Banks, Desert Rat in WWII and later in life the butcher known by many people at Meir Heath Mill House Shop. The sign over the shop at Grindley Lane, Meir Heath was 'Ernest Banks and Son'.

Most people know it as the Hill Top Chinese takeaway now, but there is a lot of history surrounding the building and the people who lived there.

Just before Christmas 2008, I had a phone call from a gentleman who said that he had a painting I might be interested in. He explained that it was a painting of the Windmill at Meir Heath dated 1902 and that his father Ernest Banks had bought it for his mother May. The artist was Lawton, who had lived in Sandon Road. As you can see, it is a beautiful painting and shows very clearly the boat cap and old sails still in place.

In January, Tony and I went to Yarnfield to visit John Banks and his wife Lorraine, daughter Jennifer and son Geoffrey. John had married Lorraine in 1982 and lived in Longton before moving to Yarnfield. John is an engineer and Lorraine a teacher and both enjoy history.

John said, *"One of the things I loved to do was to play on the fields near to the shop before the housing estate was built. There was a pit pony in the field and I loved to go and see it. It belonged to the people who lived at the bottom of our garden. My other favourite playground was the grass on the windmill before it was tarmacked over. The stretch at the back of the mill was a lovely play area for us children and the TA huts were still there at that point. Finding a mortar bomb and not realising how dangerous it might be, I took it into the house to the horror of my father.*

When the television was first tried out up at the windmill, the company brought outside-broadcast vans there to use when televising football matches or other local events. Many of you will remember the Meir aerodrome. This was another place I liked to visit. The winch trucks for the gliding club fascinated me and it was an interesting place near to where I lived.

I think Mrs Parker kept the electrical shop, which later became Regency Fashions ladies dress shop. There was a gentlemen's outfitters, Luke Smart, which became a restaurant later. Bradbury's petrol station, garage and shop were demolished and a new filling station built, which later became a car wash. The Post Office was on Sandon Road where the Bargain Booze area is now."

In 1950, John's father had a bathroom put in the house. His father also decided that a good freezer room was needed and a refrigerated room was constructed. The underground passage to the windmill was blocked up but John said that the door could be seen – an archway in the cellar indicated that the tunnel to the windmill was not very deep underground. Settles (shelves) were still in the cellar from when it had been a beer house. There was a yard and garden, and the premises had solid fuel heating. Tony and I enjoyed our visit to meet John Banks and had much pleasure from seeing the painting.

Dorothy Bestwick

Mrs D Bestwick, Treasurer

Dorothy Bestwick is certainly one of the hardest workers on the Windmill Preservation Group Committee. Her enthusiasm for the project is infectious and she has over the years helped to raise quite a lot of money.

Having lived in The Dusty Miller building for many years may well account for her interest in Meir Heath and its history. The building is now Hill Top Cottage, the Chinese takeaway, but over the years has served the people of Meir Heath and its locality in many ways.

The 11th of January 1980 was a date which Dorothy remembers well. Leaving Leek and moving into Mill House, Dorothy's first memory of the building was "it was bitterly cold in there". When she moved into the then butcher's shop with Tom, her husband, and Richard and Andrew her two sons, Dorothy didn't realise that she was moving into such a special place. One of the oldest buildings, The Dusty Miller was situated at the top of the hill at Meir Heath in Grindley Lane, having its door on Hilderstone Road.

Land belonging to The Dusty Miller stretched across what is now the public house car park. On the deeds to the property, the land stretches right down Grindley Lane as far as Pemberton Drive. Imagine the area with no other properties. Crossing the land to the public house garden to collect water from the pump would have been the 'Dusty Miller's' task so many years ago.

When The Dusty Miller was first built, it had a tunnel under the grass leading to the Windmill. Dorothy said that the tunnel was blocked up but a door could be seen in the cellar of Mill House.

Tom and Dorothy were married and Tom worked in the shop as butcher while Dorothy worked at the MEB. One evening in 1992, Dorothy came home from her job at the MEB to find Tom feeling as if he had the flu. He told Dorothy that he had done the lawns after finishing work in the shop. At that time, Richard was 17 and Andrew 15. Tom went to bed at the usual time, still feeling as if he had the flu, but sadly in the night he passed away, having had a blood clot on his heart. Dorothy, Richard and Andrew had a great shock that night.

Knowing that his father would want him to do all he could to help the situation; Richard went to Wulfrun College, at Wolverhampton, where he learned all aspects of the butcher's trade. At that time, Malcolm worked in the shop. Richard proved to be a chip off the old block and worked hard. He won a special award and Dorothy took him to London to receive it.

Both boys enjoyed life in the butcher's shop. They knew that their father sold all meats: beef, lamb, pork chicken, turkey, and occasionally special orders for veal or venison. Sometimes pheasants were ordered and had to be plucked. I'm sure you know the tongue-twister 'I'm a pheasant plucker's mate'!

One of the meats Dorothy had never tasted was crocodile. This was a special order and Dorothy was told it was like fish. Ostrich meat was another special order and Dorothy and Richard went in 1995 to an ostrich farm in Cheshire to learn more about the meat. One of the things most people remember about Tom and Dorothy's shop was the lovely handcart placed outside on the grass. On the cart were groceries, fruit and vegetables, bedding plants and flowers. Our final visit was to The Dusty Miller, which is now the Hill Top Cottage Chinese takeaway.

The present Chinese takeaway at the top of Grindley Lane, Meir Heath, has in the stone on the wall of the building, quite high up, the legend MILL HOUSE.

It is supposed that the miller sold beer from these premises as well as doing his work at the mill tower.

```
e used for the purpose of a water tower within a certain period

XCEPT AND RESERVING unto the sd Staffs. Potteries Water Works Company thr

uccors and assns full rt and liberty to lay 2 lines of water pipes under the

d footway 3 ft 6 inches in width

ND ALSO EXCEPT AND RESERVING unto the sd Staffs. Potteries Water Works Co.

hr succors and assns the rt to repair renew or relay the sd 2 lines of pipes

s and when it shd from time to time become necy so to do

ND ALSO EXCEPT AND RESERVING a rt of foot and barrow way for the sd Staffs.

otteries Water Works Co. its succors and assns and its and thr tenants

gents servants and workmen to and from the sd windmill over and along the

d footway 3 ft 6 inches in width All wch sd exceptions and reservons were

ore parly mentd in the sd Conveyance of the 23rd March 1908

ame (except and reserved as afsd)

          UNTO the Pr in fee simple

               DULY EXECUTED by the Vrs & ATTESTED.

ED of this date the sd JOHN JOULE & SONS LTD. (thrnar old "the Company")

 the context so admits include thr succors and assns) of the one pt and

     2.
```

OFFICIAL CERTIFICATE

It is hereby certified that the Official Search applied for has been made up to the the date given on the Official Stamp below.

The Result is as follows:—

Names and addresses	Nature of registration	Date and reference number of registration	Situation of land	
			County	Parish or Place or District
JOHN JOULE AND SONS LIMITED of:- The Brewery Stone, Stafford.	LC D(ii)	1932 28.Apl. No.32216	Stafford	Meir
	LC C(iv)	1949 26.Oct. No.55480	Stafford	Meir Stoke on Trent

there leadg towards Milhorne and Blythe Marsh ALL wch sd
ppty thrnbefore desobd contd 1a. 2r. 9⅞p. or thrbts and was
more parly delineated and described in the plan drawn on a
Conveyance dtd 7th May 1914 and md btn Alton and Co. Ltd. of
the one pt and the sd H.P. Embrey of the or pt and surrounde
by a blue line
EXCEPT AND RESERVING out of the sd ppty the Windmill and a small pce of ls
contd in a circle described about the sd Windmill measuring 10 ft from the
base of the same to the circumference of the sd circle the position of wch
sd prems was shown on the sd plan and thereon coloured pink TOGR with (by
way of grant and not of exception) the benefit so far as the Vrs can grant
the same of the covt by the Staffs. Potteries Water Works Co. contd in a
Conveyance dtd 23rd March 1908 and md btn the sd Alton and Co. Ltd. of the
one pt and the sd Staffs. Potteries Water Works Co. of the other pt to cov
in the two lines of pipes under the footway 3 ft 6 inches wide coloured
green on the plan drawn on those presents and to erect and maintain an iro
fence at least 4 ft 6 inches high round the sd plot of land being the site
of the Windmill and the land surrounding the same coloured pink on the sd
plan drawn on those presents and convd to the sd Staffs. Potteries Water
Works Co. by the said Conve of the 23rd March 1908
AND ALSO with the benefit so far as the Vrs old grant the same of the prov
contd in the sd Conveyance of the 23rd March 1908 for repurchasing the pre

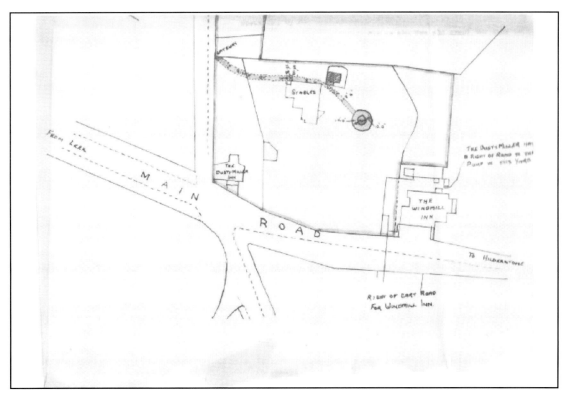

Plan of The Dusty Miller *(By kind permission of D Bestwick)*

Letter from Barbara Wild, Windmill Hill

Here is a lovely letter from Barbara Wild with information concerning the war years.

I have been living in the Meir Heath/Rough Close area for 75 years and I remember the windmill looking like the picture in the poster. The sails and capping were removed during the war as they were thought to be unsafe.

During the war, I was one of five people who used to do night shifts in the windmill. We had to listen for enemy planes circling over the area, and receive and send messages over the radio to our headquarters based in Stone. One night, a plane did fly very low and crash-landed in the fields down Hartwell Lane.

I hope something can be done to restore the Windmill to something like it used to be. It was quite a landmark at one time and could be so once again. These listed buildings should be saved, not left to fall down through neglect.

Yours sincerely, B Wild

Letter from Margaret Leach to Gill Swift

Thank you for your information about the Meir Heath Windmill Group. My grandfather, James Brookes, who lived at the Poplars Farm, Meir Heath, used to take his corn to the windmill to be ground many years ago, and my mother remembered the sails on it. As a very young child, I remember the roof, which looked rather like an upturned rowing boat. Unfortunately I am 88 this year and have had a stroke which has disabled my right side, hence the use of a very old typewriter and one finger left hand, so please excuse all the mistakes. Unfortunately will not be able to help you, though I am very interested and would appreciate hearing how you progress.

Good luck to you all, M Leach

Bill Durose at School assembly

Information Written by
Emma Flannagan (Age 10)

Emma Flannagan, age 10
(By kind permission of Mary Flannagan)

Meir Heath Windmill about 1900

The Doomsday Book made no reference to Meir Heath but mentions its neighbouring villages of Fulford, Moddershall and Kibblestone. In those days, Meir Heath was known as Maer Heath. By the end of the 17th century, Meir Heath was one of three places in North Staffordshire to have a furnace for iron smelting, an important industry in those days. An early landmark in Meir Heath was the windmill, near the crossroads. It was in use before 1840. It had a wheel arm which enabled the head of the mill and the blades to be oriented to suit the wind direction. The late Mr W H Key of the village store, the oldest inhabitant, writing in 1956, remembers it being in use. He recalls the miller spreading the canvas over the sails, prior to setting it in motion by hand. This miller was also the licensee of the local inn in the premises now occupied by Fred Miller Butchers, hence the name 'The Dusty Miller'. At Black Lake, a brother cleaning his gun accidently shot his sister. He ran away and was never heard of again. Later at the same house, the new owner of the property sank a well into which he fell and died. In medical emergencies, a doctor had to be summoned from Longton. Until 1880, two pairs of toll gates were sited at Meir Heath crossroads, levying a charge of 3 old pennies per wheeled vehicle. The first village shop was located in a house, High Croft, Windmill Hill.

School Visit

The Chairman and Secretary went to talk about the Windmill Project at Forsbrook Primary School and enjoyed the assembly. Mr B Durose, the head teacher, offered to organise a dance with his Band 'Fuzzy Logic'. Everyone enjoyed the evening and more money was raised for the fund.

The Committee are very grateful to Mr Durose and the Rotary members for all their support.

John Boucher, Millwright

The next item is an email from Mr John Boucher, Millwright, telling of his concern about the bands on the outside of the mill.

Meir Heath Mill – Structural Report – Urgent Action Required (2009)

During my site inspection I noted particularly the poor state of the three iron bands around the exterior of the tower. These were installed to resist the outwards thrust of the contained water when it was converted to a water tower in 1908. They do not now serve any structural function. They are badly corroded, and the lowest one in particular has a section missing and is no longer self-supporting. It is held most precariously by a few small nails driven into the brickwork joints. It could fall off all the way round at any moment, and possibly land in the car-park area.

I strongly advise that the bottom band be removed immediately on safety grounds, and that the two other bands should also be removed. I feel that the owners, M and B, should be advised of the situation and make the necessary arrangements. If you wish, I could contact them directly on your behalf.

I have spoken about this to the Conservation Officer, Penny McKnight, who advises that a listed building application is required (to be submitted by M and B) but that this should not cause undue delay. My own opinion is that it would be best to remove the bands altogether and not replace them, as they are not required structurally and have no relevance to its original use as a windmill. It would also remove the risk of further iron staining to the brickwork in future years. This would have to be part of the listed building application.

I am now preparing my report and should be able to submit next week when I have completed a few diagrams.

Information about the Area from Alfred Oakes to Gill Swift (2006)

Meir Heath at War

England stood alone against the might of the German army. No America, no Russia to help us. The enemy now only 21 miles away by sea, the imminent threat of invasion became real as enemy forces massed around Calais on the French coast. So it was under this threat that the British War Cabinet called upon the civilian population, men too old or too young for military service, to form a Civil Defence Force. This was named the Local Defence Volunteers (LDV) – Look Duck Vanish was the nickname. This later became the Home Guard. This formation was to assist the regular army in defence of our cities, towns, villages and ports.

The Home Guard

One such group of LDVs came together and were based at The Windmill Pub at Meir Heath. The old windmill, and Meir Heath itself, being over 830 feet above sea level, became an ideal observation post. It gave views of the countryside for miles around. Soon the name LDV was changed to the Home Guard. Most weekends, and evenings in the summer, the men paraded in the grounds of the old mill and pub. Some had uniforms, and old rifles were issued. The volunteers drilled, marched and enacted mock skirmishes in the surrounding countryside, lanes, fields and hedgerows. The Home Guard did role-play events. For instance, they commandeered a local farmer's milk float after hiding in the hedge. They did this as a training exercise, testing the rest of the troops.

The Meir Heath Home Guard's commanding officer was Mr Oswald Garrett who, in his working life, was the manager of a pottery in Longton. A typical English gentleman, he was always smartly dressed in civilian clothes or uniform. He wore plus-fours to work, smoked a pipe and had a game of crib in the pub. He was punctual, travelling to work on the same bus at the same time every day. You could set your watch by him. With a military moustache and in uniform, he looked like the typical British officer. Captain Garnett, as his title was, lived about 100 yards inside the boundary marking Stoke-on-Trent from Fulford parish in Sandon Road. I think he had served for a short time in the army near the end of the 1914–18 war. His second in command was Mr Charles Edwards, who was a partner in the pottery company of Cartwright and Edwards, Longton. The two men enjoyed each other's company and paired up for games of crib in The Windmill Pub. They would consult their watches to walk home together, as their homes were not more than 300 yards apart. Of course, the population of Meir Heath was nowhere near as numerous as it is today. Most weekends, a small contingent of Home

Guard manned a wooden command post at the rear of The Windmill Pub, two men taking turns to stand guard, two hours on duty and four hours off, throughout the weekend.

War Workers of Meir Heath

During the week, a lot of people did war work, some being collected by buses to work in a large munitions factory at Swynnerton. During this dangerous process of filling shells and bombs, accidents inevitably happened, causing injury and death.

In 1939, the Rootes car company in Liverpool, under government direction, built an aircraft factory off Grindley Lane, near to Blythe Bridge. A small one was also built further up Grindley Lane towards Meir Heath. The first planes assembled there were Blenheim bombers. Later on, they also built Beaufighters. On completion, they were towed by tractors up to two large flight sheds, where they were tested before being ferried off to different units anywhere in the country. These flight sheds were situated on the edge of the old Meir aerodrome, now called Meir Park. The workforce for this aircraft factory was drawn from Meir Heath, the surrounding area and Stoke-on-Trent. Many employees commuted by train, which called at the numerous large and small stations dotted throughout the area. They alighted at Blythe Bridge railway station to walk the short distance to the factory.

In a field close by the smaller of the two factories, number 8, further up Grindley Lane, a military camp was set up with the usual Nissan huts and guard posts etc. This area now supports a small garden centre. Through this transit camp passed the forces of various nations: Poles, Free French, American, Dutch, British, and even enemy prisoners of war. It was not a large camp and its occupants never stayed for any length of time. There seemed to be a regular rotation of allied personnel through its huts.

Auxiliary Fire Service (AFS)

Another group of volunteers doing their bit for the war effort, collected from the local people, was the AFS. These volunteers were recruited by word of mouth in shops, pubs and workplaces. They were based in a house further down Windmill Hill, next to Grundy's Lane. Mr Irving, one of a family who owned Paragon China in Sutherland Road, Longton, was in charge of the squad. The mobility of the squad was enhanced by the gift of a Ford V8 Pilot car, provided by donations from local people. This car was adapted to carry ladders and tow a fire pump. My brother, Stan Oakes, was a member of the crew, which came under the operational control of Stone Fire Service. The AFS sometimes paraded with the Horne Guard on the Windmill car park. The Meir Heath AFS occupied the first floor in the Windmill and the ARP (Air Raid Precautions) group was on the ground floor. The ARP was to keep a sharp look out for any incendiary devices that might fall in the area. ARP personnel also kept watch from the top of important buildings throughout many large cities. At the beginning of hostilities, when the air-raid sirens sounded, we rushed to our Anderson Shelters in the garden, fearing the worst. After a while, when nothing of danger was imminent, we stayed, perhaps foolishly, in the comfort of our own homes.

There were occasions when we stood on Shooter Hills, watching the anti-aircraft fire over Birmingham and Coventry during night raids by enemy bombers.

Some bombs were dropped in the Stoke-on-Trent area, causing loss of life and injury and damage to property. The nearest one to Meir Heath dropped in the garden of a house in Grindley Lane, not far from the aircraft factory, Number 10. It caused little damage.

On the western side of Meir aerodrome lay a large wooded area which fronted on to Jack Ashes Lane, now Grange Road. This was considered to be a serious hazard to pilots being trained there, a number of would-be flyers and aircraft having come to grief there. All the woodland was therefore cleared. The training planes were mostly Miles Masters and Miles Majesties, but other trees in the area claimed their victims, one in Sandon Road opposite the Blue Boar cottages.

ancient lights *Light through a window which has been enjoyed for at least twenty years. The enjoyment then becomes a legal right.*

THE LEASE

The Windmill

By Henry Wadsworth Longfellow

I stand here in my place,
With my foot on the rock below,
And whichever way it may blow
I meet it face to face,
As a brave man meets his foe.

The Lease

After applying for one or two grants, our group decided that we wouldn't get help until we had a lease to the windmill.

Ian White (Knights solicitors, Newcastle) heard Tony and me on Radio Stoke one Sunday afternoon on the Good Times Show with Terry Walsh. We asked for a solicitor to help us with the details of the lease and Ian White rang in to say that he would help us sort it out. It was February 2007.

We began meetings with Ian to decide what we needed to have in the lease and we met in his rooms at Knights' offices in Newcastle, where each meeting began with us having a delicious cup of coffee. Usually, six of the Committee went, taking a list of questions and Ian would help while his secretary took the minutes of the meetings.

The company working for M&B were Eversheds of Manchester.

Emails were going back and forth between me and both solicitors, and Ian was making sure everything was as we had agreed with M&B estate manager, Mary Evans, when we met her earlier that year.

Meanwhile, we heard that Awards for All would give us a grant for £10,000 to do work to make the windmill safe, but it had to be used by 29 October 2009. This meant that things were starting to happen. Once all the conditions of the lease were agreed, Ian White rang to tell me that I would need to go to the local Commissioner for Oaths in order to be allowed to sign the lease. John Bradbeer was also invited to sign the lease on behalf of the Committee.

Newsletter Sent to All the Committee (2009)

Date	Event
26 October	*The Secretary went to Chesworth Solicitors and paid £5 to take the oath.*
26 October	*The Secretary and Chairman took the documents to Ian White, our solicitor.*
5 November	*Eversheds, their solicitors, sent back the lease stating that it had a typographical error! (11.15am)*
5 November	*Our solicitor's trainee, Chris Kay, rang to ask if John Bradbeer and the Secretary would go to Newcastle and sign again the corrected lease. John was at his snooker club so his wife phoned him and he was at Newcastle by noon.* *The Secretary and Chairman arrived just after John and went to see Chris Kay. John signed again and then went home.* *Chris Kay took The Secretary and Chairman to a Commissioner for Oaths in Newcastle where the Secretary swore again! But still had to pay another £5.00.* *Mary Evans, M and B, sent word to say that the furniture would be moved out of the mill and that they would then complete. Time passed!* *The Secretary sent more emails to Hannah Beko, Eversheds, asking for things to be sorted out as soon as possible but to no avail. The builder was put on hold.*
18 November	*Chris Kay rang to say he had just received the lease and would post it.*
19 November	*the lease arrived. The Secretary noticed that it was signed by her and by John Bradbeer but not by M and B people.*

	The Secretary rang Chris Kay, who rang Hannah Beko, who then sent the copy signed. Two people had signed for M and B and they had dated the page 25/8/09. Why had we waited until now? The furniture had gone from the mill.
20 November	*the Chairman went to collect the **key**.*
21 November	*the Chairman went to get a spare key cut for the builder.*
23 November	*Phil Hancock started work.*
30 November	*M and B to fix electric supply – two days' work, £1,500.*
30 November	*celebration at Florence Sports and Social Club.*

Terms of the Lease

Principal Rent	*A Peppercorn (if demanded)*
Rent Commencement Date	*The Term of Commencement*
Term Commencement Date	*1st June 2009*
Break Dates	*Fifth, Tenth, Fifteenth, Twentieth Anniversary of the Term Commencement Date*

Our Visit to the Record Office in Hanley

Christopher Kirk

Looking at the old newspaper on microfiche at Hanley Record Office, Anthony found an item about Christopher Kirk from Etruria. He was advertising for a miller to work at Meir Heath Windmill. Finding the Victoria County History of Staffordshire, Volume 8, JG Jenkins edition, we discovered interesting information on pages 194 to 205.

"Minton was using a water power for grinding his materials from 1796 but in 1819 he installed a 24-horse-powered steam engine built by Christopher Kirk. Margaret, wife of Christopher Kirk, was buried in St John the Baptist churchyard, Burslem, March 1848, aged 78. Christopher Kirk of Etruria was buried 20 July 1855, aged 80.

The document showing the Quarter Session Records of 1822 has, in item 11, details of Christopher Kirk, millwright. (Thanks to Steve Birks' potteries.org site for this interesting information.) Pigot's Directory 1828/9 has a fascinating list of occupations and it was here that Anthony found, under BRASS FOUNDERS, Christopher Kirk.

The Staffordshire Advertiser (Saturday 12 January 1827)
TO MILLERS
WANTED immediately a steady, active single MAN as a miller apply to Mr WALKER MAER Heath Windmill – Mill near Stone Staffordshire. N.B. None need apply who cannot produce a desirable character from their last situation.
(This is how it was printed!)

The Staffordshire Advertiser (Saturday 4 August 1837)
Maer Heath Windmill Upper Lane End to be let with -- --- that capital WINDMILL in good repair with Kiln new house garden, stables. Outbuilding together with about seven acres of land. For Further particulars refer to Tom Browser.
On the premises. Letters to be post paid.

The Staffordshire Advertiser (7 October 1848)
TO MILLERS
TO BE LET and maybe entered upon immediately, a WINDMILL most eligibly situated at MEAR HEATH in the Parish of Stone, a short distance only from Longton, Staffordshire Potteries.
The Mill contains two pairs French stones, one pair meal stones, one pair of shelling stones, dressing machine and drying kiln.
The above in excellent repair.
Also to LET a MILLER'S HOUSE with seven acres of good turf LAND.
For further particulars apply to MR CHRISTOPHER KIRK IRON WORKS, ETRURIA, and Staffordshire

The Staffordshire Advertiser (Saturday 30 August 1848)
CORN MILL and BEER HOUSE TO BE LET and entered upon immediate.
WINDCORNMILL situated Maer Heath near Longton, together with BEER HOUSE and about seven acres of LAND attached. Apply to C KIRK, Esq. Etruria or to the present Tenant on the premises.

The Corn Laws

The Corn Laws were first introduced in Britain in 1804 when the landowners, who dominated Parliament, sought to protect their profits by imposing a duty on imported corn. During the Napoleonic Wars it had not been possible to import corn from Europe. This led to an expansion of British wheat farming and to high bread prices.

Farmers feared that when the war came to an end in 1815, the importation of foreign corn would lower prices. This fear was justified and the price of corn fell from 126s. 6d. a quarter in 1812 to 65s. 7d. three years later. British landowners applied pressure on members of the House of Commons to take action to protect the profits of the farmers. Parliament responded by passing a law permitting the import of foreign wheat free of duty only when the domestic price reached 80 shillings per quarter (8 bushels). During the passing of this legislation, the Houses of Parliament had to be defended by armed troops against a large angry crowd.

This legislation was hated by the people living in Britain's fast-growing towns who had to pay these higher bread prices. The industrial classes saw the Corn Laws as an example of how Parliament passed legislation that favoured large landowners. The manufacturers in particular were concerned that the Com Laws would result in a demand for higher wages.

There was a dreadful harvest in 1816. This caused bread prices to increase rapidly. This was followed by industrial unrest as workers demanded higher wages in order to pay for the increased food prices. As well as strikes, there were food riots all over Britain.

The Corn Laws had an important political impact on Manchester. It was one of the main reasons why a group of middle-class moderate reformers began meeting at the home of John Potter. It also influenced working-class radicals and the Com Laws were one of the main issues that were to be addressed at the meeting that they had organised at St. Peter's Field on 16 August, 1819.

Grain Rents Document

593/G/1/12

Grain Rents. Rents for farms were regulated by the average price for wheat in England and Wales from the 1st day of January 1825 to the 1st day of January 1826.

Annual rent in Lightwood for George Ferneyhough was £90. For John Proctor it was £135. The wheat price was 80 shillings a quarter or £4. As the price of wheat went down to 56/6d (£2 16s 6d) in 1827 to 1828, the rent decreased. In 1833 to 1834, the price of wheat was £2 6s 2d a quarter. In 1837 it was £2 4s 8d. The price of wheat started to rise again and by 1849 it was £2 18s 4d.

Leslie Thomas Bartlam – Interview 2010

At his home in Woodside Drive, Leslie Bartlam invited us in to talk to him about his life. He was born in 1920 so next year, on 11 February 2011, he will be 91. The first thing we saw in Leslie's home was a framed photograph on the wall showing details of a certificate of Dunkirk and Les was very proud of that, telling us all about his life in the army. At the age of 19, Les joined the Territorial Engineers. Living in Sandford Hill, Stoke-on-Trent, he went to the Hanley Group. After about ten weeks training, he was sent to France in 1939 as part of the 292 Royal Engineers Field Company. First port of call was the west coast at La Baille and then later to Lille.

His work involved building concrete pill boxes along the Belgian border to be used for gun emplacements. Les said that he didn't think that they would ever be used. Moving on to Brussels in Belgium, he worked there until it was time to move back to Dunkirk in May 1940. Les stayed just outside Dunkirk until 1 June 1940 at La Panne and was fortunate to be picked up by a minesweeper. He remembers climbing netting to get onto the ship.

Les said *"I certainly knew how to look after myself. You had to."* Arriving back at Sheerness up the Thames Estuary, he went to Portsmouth. At West Wittering, men were regrouped and worked in shifts. Les had the job of cutting up broken railway lines and they were put on the beach as an obstruction in case of a German invasion.

Next place for Les to go was Gosport, where he was seconded to the Fleet Air Arm maintenance unit and transferred to the Royal Army Ordnance Corps. After this, Les went to REM (Royal Electrical Mechanical Engineers) stationed at Fife, where he stayed until 1942, when he moved out to Ceylon (Sri Lanka) where he maintained anti-aircraft guns.

His life in Ceylon was different. While there, he lived in a palm hut made of bamboo frames with palm leaves as a roof. In the Far East, Les saw the Burma Railway and the famous Tiger Balm Gardens in 1943. He still remembers the terrible monsoon, with humid hot sticky days living in that part of the world. He remembers his diet was mainly curry and rice and American-issue tack biscuits and tins of spam. All the water had to be boiled and great care taken all the time. At this time he received £7 a week and said it was more than a staff sergeant received. At Assam, the local people came out over the mountains with their elephants before the Japanese arrived. After the war, Les came back to Staffordshire and went to work for T&J Bartlem, his father's business. His grandfather had started the business earlier with 150 horses and carts and even took tramlines as far away as Huddersfield.

When private companies were nationalised and called British Road Services, Leslie's family had Meir Heath Garage. Leslie and his brother Bill had their homes built

behind the garage. The garage men did repairs and were dealers for Esso petrol.

Leslie showed us a photograph of himself and his wife Irene, whom he met at Nottingham. He has a son Craig and a daughter Lesley, and grandchildren Stephanie, Philipa and Adam.

We discussed the Meir Heath area where Jack Bartlam owned six and half acres of land and Les said: *"Oswald Coup bought the land from my father. We lived in a house called Isleworth. All fields, and Oswald Coup built houses there, but before he built the houses, he built Meir Heath Primary School in Golborn Drive. The roads are Hollies Drive, Willow Drive, Woodside Drive, Heather Drive and many more houses in the area. What good clean air there is here at Meir Heath. It's the highest point, you know."* Thank you, Leslie, for letting us spend an interesting afternoon with you.

An Artist at Home – Mr Roy Deakin

Living in the area for so many years, Roy is full of facts about Meir Heath. Before we start talking, I take photographs of Roy's latest painting, which is of a beautiful violin in the same style as the one done on a door at Chatsworth House, Derbyshire.

"If the Duke of Devonshire can have a violin painted on his door, I can have one on my door," comments Roy. Son David Deakin and daughter-in-law Rita, and grandsons James, aged 19, and Oliver, aged 15, love to visit Roy and encourage him in his art work. David has helped Roy with the interesting map of Meir Heath.

When we started to talk about the area, Roy said, *"Do you know where Starvation Nurseries are?"* "No I'm afraid I don't," I said.

"Well, they are on Knenhall Lane, a very cold, bleak place near to the Wheatsheaf Inn at Moddershall. There used to be a building for the workers. Land girls worked there. It was owned by a family and Italian prisoners of war worked there, growing cabbages for the war effort. A family named Dales lived at the farm along Hilderstone Road near to the strawberry farm." Roy went on to say that there was another farm and a slaughter house opposite. *"It smelled of bones and was not very pleasant. Further along Hilderstone Road was the council tip for Stone Rural Area.*

An avenue of trees was on the side past the tip by Hill's Nursery. Hill's was by the crossroads. The legend states that the gibbets were near there, where people were hanged.

I remember Black Lake Plantation towards Fulford, near to Stallington Lane. Some think of it as Diamond Wood because of the shape on the map."

Along Hilderstone Road was the old Toll House and Roy remembered his grandfather Deakin moving the bricks from the toll house and taking them to Shooters Hills farm in Lightwood Road. The bricks were used as hardcore for a road leading to the marl pit where clay was extracted to make red quarry tiles.

Louise Austin married Stan Hales and lived in the tollgate house. (That is roughly where Martins shop is

Barbara and Roy Deakin

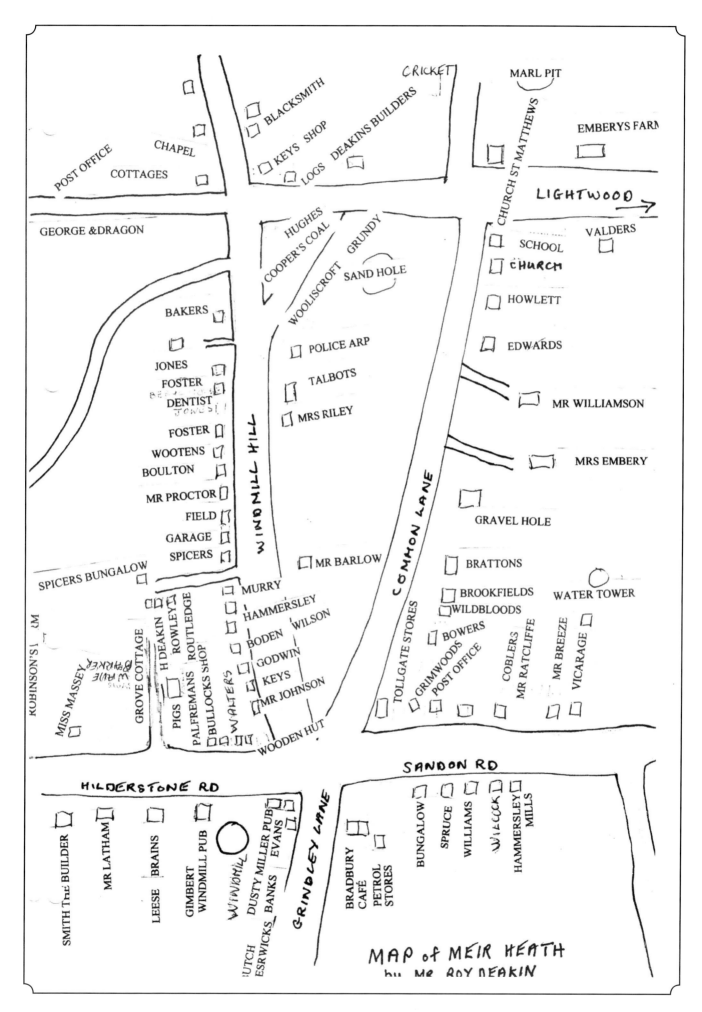

Map of Meir Heath as it was when Roy was a Boy

Oliver and James Deakin

Roy Deakin's paintings

now.) It was situated practically on the edge of the road and next to what used to be Regency Fashions and the Stanier family.

Previously Regency Fashions was Mr Parker's television shop. Roy bought a 12-inch TV which had a black and white picture, as early televisions had.

What we see as Bargain Booze was Mrs Nixon's Post Office. There was a café opposite the Post Office, but not kept for long as a cafe. Mrs Bradbury had the cafe. There were petrol pumps but no garage.

A footpath leading to Rough Close, Windmill Hill and Leadendale Lane could be seen among the trees. *"Jennifer's Wood was named after Mr Hill's daughter and did have some beautiful trees,"* said Roy. As he talked about Hilderstone Road, Roy spoke about the football pitch there, near to Poplars stables and livery, which had been Mr Robinson's home. Mrs Massey lived at the other toll house and it can be seen on the photograph. Andy's butchers used to be Palfreymans, next to Goodfellows, which had been Fiddlers' shop. Deryn's Hair Salon and lovely old cottages sit in a group together.

Moments restaurant sits at the end of the road and is noted for its good food.

Tony Swift and Roy Deakin go to Look Around Meir Heath

Tony Swift took Roy Deakin in the car for a ride around Meir Heath and along the Hilderstone Road. Roy has such a splendid memory and knows so much about the area. Starting at the windmill, Roy said that there had been a five-bar gate by the entrance to the grounds of the windmill with a wicker gate by the side. All of what is now the car park had been a large field of grass. When Roy was a boy, he often saw horses kept in the stables at the back of the public house, and usually bicycles left at the front of the windmill. As they left the windmill car park, Roy said to Tony:

"On the left we can see Mr Latham's house next to Mr Smith's, the builder's house. Soon we shall pass the lane where the Evans family lived. Oakes organ business is just near here on the left, near to Reynolds. Just after Golborn Avenue is a lovely house where Mr Salmon, from Salmon & Jones Garage (Fenton), lived. Jack and Brenda Bissell lived in that house and then Dr and Mrs Brian Harvey. Further along is a house called NONSUCH that makes me think of Walkers Toffee, which local folks know as Nonsuch. Lovely sweets."

Roy continued:

"Down the Hilderstone Road on the left is Willow Lane and Meir Heath Cricket Club. There used to be trees all along that stretch of road. Moving on until we reach Black Lake Lodge Nursing Home, which I believe once belonged to Mr Beswick. Nearby was the cottage where John Myatt lived. Reaching the crossroads, to the right is Moddershall Oaks

and Moddershall Oaks Health Club, a lovely place to visit for a meal. Charlie Dale has a house on the corner surrounded by beautiful trees. Then Blacklake Pool and Blacklake Inn. A poultry farm was situated on the left along the road, a bungalow and farm where the slaughter house was. The building is still there. A caravan site is just behind the trees and nearby is an old milestone."

Arriving at the Spotgate pub, Tony parked his car and the two men went to look more closely at the pub. On the way back to Meir Heath, Tony said that he remembered seeing micro lights taking off to fly from nearby fields and Roy pointed out the field that the people knew as the Gibbets. Hills Nursery is at the end of that section of road. John Hill had first started the business and was well known in the area. Roy said that when John died, his ashes were scattered in the woods by the cricket field.

The Heart of England Nursery is now called Mount Nursery and is situated at the junction where one road leads to Fulford and one to Stone. As they drove back towards Blacklake Inn, which Roy knows as the Wheatsheaf Inn, at last the rain stopped. On the way, they passed the house called Jakaranda, where years ago the family kept ponies.

The Poplars riding school used to be a farm and Roy said that during the Second World War, cheese was stored in the farm loft. People used to go and turn the cheese to be sure it matured properly. Roy continued: *"At this time, none of the estates were built. Bill Burton had a farm and Robinsons had a farm, and they supplied the milk round during the war. They had a big house built near to the Wheatsheaf Inn. Nearby was Myatt's Cottage. Their daughter, Joan, died when she was quite young, about 13. She had meningitis. I was very lucky when I was ill with it. I lost the use of my arm and was given a new drug called M&B tablets. They were the latest tablets out. No penicillin then. Old Doctor Oliver, not Keith Oliver his son, looked after me until I was better."*

If you were a resident of Meir Heath when Roy was young, you would need a Stuart Turner water pump to boost water into your attic or loft because the reservoir was not high enough to gravity-feed your system. Water for the area came from Meir Pumping Station.

Roy's family were well known in the area as builders and Mr Degg engaged the company to build a house on Windmill Hill, a very imposing house built high up on the hill (now a day nursery for children). Before that house was built, Roy used to go hunting for rabbits with his dad in the field where the house was later built. Roy thinks the house was built in the 1960s. Mr Degg kept his racehorses there.

We don't realise how hard life could be, all those years ago. Roy went on to tell about the fact that if anyone was ill in the area, a district nurse would be sent for and had to cycle from Stone. Some years later, Nurse Radcliffe was appointed and lived on Hilderstone Road, later moving to Common Lane in a lovely bungalow. Her husband kept the cobblers' shop in a wooden hut, which was near where the dentist is now. As we all stood on the car park at the Windmill; Roy talked of Mr Gimbert and his family. Mr Gimbert was landlord of the Windmill Inn. When he was a child, Roy used to go on the swing boats on the grass by the side of the pub. It was always a favourite pub of the locals and visitors came from the Potteries for a day out at the weekend.

Also in the area were Embery's farmers near to Rough Close. They had a bakery in Fenton. Bread was delivered by horse and van, yes van! Shafts were attached to the horse and to the van. Still thinking about Lightwood Road, Roy remembered Mr Gotham, who had a small garden and sold tomatoes and plants. This was near to the Brickmaker's Arms public house and Shooters Hills house and caves, which belonged to Mr Bailey who had a colour works there.

I am very grateful to Mr Roy Deakin and his family for all their help with the Windmill Project. Whenever there is an event, Roy always gives his support and encouragement and I, on behalf of the Meir Heath Preservation Group, thank him for all his help.

J. Deakin's Letter

Inside the Windmill Inn

Mrs Brenda Allan

PARTICULARS.

LOT 1.

A Double-fronted Bay Window Villa

Known as "THE POPLARS, situate at Meir Heath.

It contains, Entrance Hall (laid with Minton Tiles), Drawing and Dining Rooms, Kitchen, Back Kitchen (with Copper), Pantry and Larder, Coal House, Four Bedrooms and Box Room, Bath Room (H. & C.) and W.C., and Cylinder Cupboard.

There are substantial Farm Buildings, including a Brick and Tiled Range (with Tying for 11 Cows and 8 Calves), with Loft over; A Pigstye, Loose Box and Trap House.

Another Range includes, Stabling for 8 Horses (with Loft over).

A Wood and Corrugated three-bay Hay Barn.

There is a Garden and several Fields of Old Turf Land, the whole containing

32 acres 3 rood 7 perches

or thereabouts, as more particularly shown below :

SCHEDULE.

No on Ord. Map (2nd Edition)	Description			Area
204 (pt.) Turf	...	...	...	1.350
224 Turf	...	...	...	3.222
225 (pt.) Residence, Buildings, etc.	...	...	...	.564
230 Turf	...	...	...	5.930
231 Turf	...	...	...	5.331
232 Turf	...	...	...	3.215
233 Turf	...	...	...	3.869
249 Turf	...	...	...	5.193
250 Turf	...	...	...	4.118
				A. 32.792

The Property is in the occupation of the Owner, Mr. A. J. BROOKES, and VACANT POSSESSION will be given on completion.

This is a particularly desirable Property for occupation, lying on a good Road, just outside the Borough Boundary of Stoke-on-Trent.

Town Water is laid on and the Telephone is connected.

The Property is most convenient for anyone having Business in the Potteries.

Our Supporters

Many people have supported events presented by the Preservation Group.
Here are a few photographs to show those events.

The ladies from the Chinese takeaway – our group wishes to thank the owners who kindly supported the Windmill Wacky Races
(Photo A Swift)

R Bradbury, C Bradbury, O Swift and D Swift

Edinburgh Mill Fashion Show at Trentham (2011)
– Stephanie Shingler, Beryl Lancaster and Jeannie Farrinond *(Photo A Swift)*

Dog show and Summer Fair held at the Windmill (2011)
– Christian Bradbury, D Swift, L Swift, G Bagnall, M Rushton and A Bagnall

The Team at the dentists - J.Kocierz (BDS), J Hughes (BDS), LKoceirz, C Stanier, J Fawkes, S Morris, V Tooth and A Peebles

Goodfellaz - G Dipiazza, G Sullivan and L Taylor - Hilderstone Road

The hairdressers at Meir Heath Salon, Hilderstone Road, Meir Heath -
Cathy Willock, Deryn Reynolds and Annette Pettitt, Celebrating 40 years in business at Meir Heath

Andrew and Stewart Sim at their shop, ANDY'S, Hilderstone Road, Meir Heath
- great supporters of the Windmill Project - in business for 17 years (2012)

Celebration Day 2010 - G Swift, A Swift, the Mayor of Stafford, Cllr Millichap and the Mayoress, Mrs Milllichap

A & G Bagnall with the celebration cake they presented to the group

The group at the celebration

In the mill - M Flannagan, M Levie, J Bradbeer, M Upton and N Morley

K Williams & A Swift

G Swift, the Mayor & P Hancock

A Oakes, M Flannagan, Adam the Landlord, the Mayor (Cllr Millichap), A Swift & G Swift at the celebration party

A Swift explains how the project was organised

S Beardmore, M Upton, M Flannagan and N Mould

S Ebrill, M Upton and G Ebrill

M T Walsh (Radio Stoke presenter)

M Flannagan, granddaughter Zara and Deputy Mayoress Mrs Green
(Photo D Beardmore)

Lady Mayoress of Stafford receiving flowers from M Flannagan's granddaughter, Zara

A and G Swift with the Forever Friends dolls they take to meetings, showing the visitors the singing puppets

Meir Heath Primary School children visit

Ladder in the mill

The Deputy Mayor and Mayoress of Stone with the celebration cake

T Walsh (Radio Stoke) and A Swift

A Haymonds (Ibstock Cory Trust) with Chairman A Swift *(Photo G Swift)*

The Stoneagers singing group with conductor Pam Sinclair and The Mayor and Mayoress of Stafford
– the group entertained the audience with a medley of lovely songs and a special song about a mouse in the windmill

The Essential Mix came to help us raise money by presenting a Music Hall at Rough Close and Meir Heath Village Hall
(By kind permission of D Poole)

P Hancock and N Clowes

A Haymonds, J Bradbeer, D Beardmore, G Swift and the Lady Mayoress, Mrs Millichap

P Sinclair conducting the Stoneagers Singers

Stafford Morris Men helped to raise funds (2009)

The postmaster and his wife at Rough Close and Meir Heath Post Office,
Kashir and Daljit Moore, who are great supporters of the Windmill Project *(Photo G Swift)*

Roy Deakin at home with one of his paintings *(Photo G Swift)*

T Georgio, International Hairdresser, Grindley Lane

Edinburgh Mill Fashion Show at Trentham Gardens (2010) – Jean Ward and Hellen Riley (from Australia) *(Photo A Swift)*

Children from Meir Heath Primary School visit the Windmill (2010) – Meir Heath Windmill Preservation Group invited to talk to the children *(Photo G Swift)*

Margaret Webb is a member of one of the groups who visit

Meir Heath Primary School Visit (2011)
– Gloria Ellis and Anthony Swift *(Photo G Swift)*

The group visit Meir Heath Primary School to talk about local history –
G Swift, A Swift, N Mould, C Mould, D Beardmore, A Aitchison, A Humpage, P Humpage, M Webb and D Bestwick *(Photo S Beardmore)*

Dog show (2011) – Mr and Mrs Cook with their dogs

Inside the mill *(Photo A Swift)*

Stone Townswomen's Guild invited Gill and Tony to speak to the ladies about the Windmill Project – B Bird, G Swift, P Sinclair, S Evans, A Taylor and Pam Sinclair who is holding a copy of Yates map

Stoneager Singers went to Heron Cross Senior Citizen's Club where tea was served and the visitors enjoyed the programme – A Swift and S Ebrill with two of the guests

Sandon Business and Enterprise College

Work starting on Sandon Business and Enterprise College

Miss B Hall (retired head teacher) was very helpful in sending our group a disc with many photographs of the college being built. It was hard to choose which to include.

Many thanks for the children, teachers and office staff who have helped our group with designing and printing flyers.

Our group have enjoyed meeting in the Conference Room at the College and marvel at the beautiful building.

Some of the staff of Sandon Business and Enterprise College, Sandon Road, Meir –
M Wildblood, T Podmore, P Worthy, W Horton and J Wright – thanks to P Marsden for her help

The Walking Bus – children from Meir Heath Primary School meet at the Windmill, then with teachers and parents walk to school

(Photo A Swift)

Some of the local shops at Meir Heath
(Photo A Swift)

Tolls and Turnpike Roads

This information was found concerning the Turnpike Trust Record at Stafford Record Office. (By Royal Assent 23 May 1823.)

From medieval times until the eighteenth century, the money and labour needed to maintain roads had to come from the inhabitants of the village where the road passed through. This was common law and duties collected by different authorities were not successful. Until Tudor times, local organisers were medieval units – the manor court, the Church, the guilds and borough corporations. In 1555, an Act came into force which decreed that each parish must see to its highway maintenance. Surveyors were to make local landowners give four days labour and cartage services. In 1894, a Local Government Act finally removed parish authority to new district councils.

Roads were still terrible. Travellers suffered and something had to be done. Turnpike Trusts were set up by local acts of Parliament to recoup their expenses by the levying of tolls on road users. During the period 1700–1830, hundreds of such private enterprises were set up all over England. The general Turnpike Act of 1773 encouraged the development of trusts and an improvement was soon seen. Turnpike Records are for all to see at SRO, with statements of accounts and maps showing turnpike roads, toll bars and houses. Hilderstone Road was a turnpike road and was probably used a lot by the miller of the windmill built on Hilderstone Road before 1775. A toll house was along the road near to the Poplars. Roy Deakin's memories give details concerning the toll house.

Tolls

For every horse or other beast drawing any carriage of any description the sum of three pence. For every horse, ass or mule, laden or unladen, and not drawing, the sum of one penny. For every ox, cow or head of cattle the sum of one halfpenny.

For every calf, pig, sheep or lamb the sum of one farthing. Horses and carts carrying lime for manuring pay ½ tolls. Infringement £5 fine.

N.B. Pay once a day to pass through any toll site on all of that road. Ticket to be produced. Stagecoaches or other conveyance of passengers to pay each time of passing or repassing along the said road. Double toll on Sundays.

An agreement may be made with the trustees for a yearly pass for frequent use by horses, cattle or the beasts, fee to be paid quarterly in advance. Certain additional exceptions for road-building materials, hay, straw or food to feed horses working on said road. Doctors who are visiting the sick are exempt. Rectors, vicars or curates are also exempt on Sunday along with parishioners going to or returning from church service. Mail coaches are exempt. Also exempt are beasts and wagons of His Majesty's militia as long as the soldier is in uniform

Staffordshire. **THE POTTERIES.** **Pigot & Co.'s**

page 725

BRICK & TILE MAKERS

Bourne & Hawthorn, Longport
Elkin John, Etruria
Fitchford James, Etruria
Haywood Howard & Richd (& blue tile (water pipe &c) Brownhills
Peake Thos. & Co. (& water pipes & blue & vitreous) Tunstall
Shufflebotham Robert, Tunstall
Warner James, Etruria

BRICK LAYERS

Shaw Jno. Navigation rd, Burslem
Wildig Thos. Piccadilly, Shelton

BRICK MAKERS

Brassington & Pratt, Dale's nook, Lane End
Cook Jas. Bricker's field, Lane End
Glover James, New st, Lane End
Robey Wm. & Co. New st, Lane End

BUTCHERS

Ashton Richard, High st, Lane End
Ashton Wm. High st, Lane End
Belfield Robt. Queen st, Burslem
Bradbury Wm. Chapel passage, Hanley
Cliff Richd. Newcastle st, Stoke
Cope Benj. Gt Charles st, Lane End
Eley George, Nile St, Burslem
Fielding Chas. George st, Hanley
Ford John, Newcastle st, Burslem
Green George, Lane Delph
Hall James, Wood st, Lane End
Hares Richard, Broad st, Shelton
Huson Wm. Newcastle st, Stoke
James John, High st, Hanley
Lees George, Lane Delph
Lovatt Joseph, High st, Lane End
Sargeant Cs. Upper High st, Hanley
Sargeant John, Etruria
Steele Jos. Market place, Tunstall
Turner Simon, Fenton
Turner Thomas, Mort st, Stoke

CABINET MAKERS AND UPHOLSTERERS

Betteley Hy. Liverpool rd, Burslem
Betteley John, Market pl, Hanley

CHINA MANUFACTURERS
... continued

Davenport Jno. Son & Co. Longport
Dillon Fras. & Nicholas, Cobridge
Drewry Ts. Daisy bank, Lane End
Faniker & Robinson, George st, Lane End
Folch Stephen (stone) Church st, Lane End
Gerrard Cope & Co. High st, Lane End
Handley James & Willm. Killcroft, Burslem
Hicks, Meigh & Johnson, Broad st, Shelton
Hilditch Wm. & Sons, Church st, Lane End
Jarvis Wm. Great Charles st, Lane End
Machin Jos. & Co. Nile st, Burslem
Martin Wm. Market pl, Lane End
Mason & Co. Lane Delph
Mayer & Newbold, Market pl, Lane End
Mayer Thomas, Cliffe bank, Stoke
Minton Thos. New road, Stoke
Pratt, Hassall & Gerrard, Lane Delph
Rathbone Saml. & John, Tunstall
Ridgway Jno. & Co. High st, Shelton
Ridgway Jno. & Wm. (stoke) Cauldon place
Riley Jno. & Richd. Liverpool rd, Burslem
Shaw Jno, Green dock, Lane End
Simkin Hugh, High st, Lane End
Spode Josiah, Newcastle st, Stoke
Taylor William, Hogg's lane, Lane E
Weston Geo. High st, Lane End
Yates John, Broad st, Shelton

CHYMISTS - MANUFACTURING

Birch & Joues (copperas) Shelton
Child & Treffry, Clay hill, Tunstall

CLOTHES DEALERS

Beverley David, High st, Hanley
Boothby Wm. Tontine st, Hanley
Clowes John, Lane Delph
Hulme Wm. Market pl, Burslem
Noon Benj. Market st, Lane End
Shufflebottom Dl. Broad st, Shelton
Warrin Saml. Tontine st, Hanley
Warrin Saml. Market st, Lane End

CONFECTIONERS

Beardmore Hy. Market pl, Tunstall
Birch John, Market st, Lane End
Edge Jos. St. John's sq, Burslem
Hawks John, Albion st, Shelton
Potts Jas. Newcastle st, Stoke
Travis John, Market sq, Hanley
Walker Jas. Newcastle st, Burslem
Wright John, Market pl, Hanley

COOPERS

Brown Wm. High st, Lane End
Clews James, Cliff bank, Stoke
Clews John, High st, Lane End
Houldcroft Martha, Market place, Burslem
Jenkins Geo. Union Market place, Lane End
Pass Charles, Hanover st, Burslem
Price Robt. Tontine passage, Hanley
Stanway Thos. Market st, Hanley
Trubshaw Charles, Toll st, Hanley
Whittle Wm. Liverpool rd, Burslem

CORN & FLOUR DEALERS

Appleby George, Longport
Carey Thos. & Jno. jun. (& millers) Anchor st, Lane End
Cartwright Jas. Market st, Lane End
Cholerton Thos, Etruria locks
Dawson John, Tontine st, Hanley
Downs James, Albion st, Shelton
Galley James, Market st, Burslem
Hill Caleb (flour) Market st, Lane End, Queen st, Burslem, & Stafford row, Hanley
Johnson Ralph, Market pl, Burslem
Keeling Samuel, Piccadilly, Shelton
Malpass William, Tunstall
Pratt Hy. & Thos. New road, Stoke
Shaw Ralph, HANLEY MILL

CRATE MAKERS

Austin Sampson, High st, Shelton
Baker Jno. Pack-horse la, Burslem
Bentley Geo. Dale Hall, Longport
Birks John, Church st, Stoke
Birks Samuel, High st, Lane End
Chesworth Catherine, Etruria
Cooper Thos. Dale hall, Longport
Cope William, Cobridge

12 pennies =	*1 shilling*
20 shillings =	*1 pound (£1)*
240 pence =	*1 pound (£1)*
2 half pence =	*1 penny*
4 farthings =	*1 penny*

Occupations Seen in Fulford Parish Register

1813–1817	
WEAVER 1	LABOURERS 2
INN KEEPER 4	BUTCHER 3
FARMER 24	CORDWAINER 15
GENTLEMEN 3	SERVANT 2
FISHMONGER 3	YEOMAN 3
DRUDGER 7	TAYLOR 1
MILLER 1	CARD MAKER 1
JOINER 1	STONE MASON 1
BLACKSMITH 3	ROPE MAKER 1
BRICK MAKER 2	MONEY CLERK 1
NAILOR 1	BAKER 1
COOPER 1	GAMEKEEPER 1
HORSE BREAKER 1	

1824
KEEPER OF THE TURNPIKE 1
PROPRIETOR OF THE LUNATIC ASYLUM 1
HORSE KEEPER 1
POTTER 1
GROCER 1
DRESSMAKER 1
BRAZIER 1

Definitions of Jobs

Cordwainer: *made a variety of goods from fine soft leather which originated from the Spanish city of Cordoba. The term Cordwainer dates back to the 12th century. Down through the centuries the occupation evolved into being known as a maker of luxury boots and shoes.*

Corfer: *in charge of a corf used in the process of mining ore or coal. The term corf either referred to the large corf basket used to hoist coal/ore, or to a wooden sled or wheeled wagon used to move coal or ore around inside a mine.*

Corn Chandler: *a dealer in corn. Corn Factor: bought and sold corn on behalf of others.*

Corn Meter: *a type of weights and measures inspector who ensured that the quantities of corn traded at market were accurately weighed.*

Corn Porter: *this occupation title usually refers to someone who worked at a dock. They unloaded corn from ships and moved it into storage, and vice versa.*

Swailer: *grain merchant or a person on forest of farmland who used controlled burning to manage the landscape.*

William Keeling

Mr W Keeling at work
(By kind permission of W Keeling)

It is 24 April 2009 and I have just spent a lovely afternoon in the company of Mr William Keeling. I was really amazed to meet someone aged 95, who didn't look a day over 75. What a wonderful time I had talking to Bill.

It was a good thing that I had lived in Fenton as a child because when he started talking, it turned out that Bill had lived in Fife Street near to Oldfield Street, Fenton, as a child. We both went to Queen Street School, although I went later than Bill.

Bill was born in 1914. Bill's parents, Harry and Eva Keeling, and his brother Harry lived together. As with so many families, Bill's father worked in the pottery industry as a saggar maker at Forester's, Longton. Eva was a cup handler and young Harry was also a saggar maker. (A saggar maker is a man who makes the cases in which the ware is put for firing. The cases are made from marl.) Bill's parents thought that he would be a good apprentice and so he went to train at night school as a joiner and worked for Kettles Company.

When Bill was 17, his family decided to move to Sandon Road, Meir Heath. The house in Fenton was on the corner of a row of terraced houses and Mr Birks, who had a shop, persuaded Bill's parents to sell their house to him so that he could make a larger shop.

"He begged and prayed for us to let him have the house," said Bill, and that's how they came to Meir Heath, selling their house for £400, which was a lot of money.

Working in the building trade, Bill had seen the houses in Sandon Road being built. There were not many houses there in 1928. Harry, Eva and the brothers went to look at the house. The builder was Mr Simister and the price of the house £625, a lot of money. Working for the builders, Kettles, at first, Bill told me that during the Second World War he was on a reserved occupation.

Bill met his wife Jessie at a dance in Fenton when she came along with friends to the 'Hut', which was near to Queen Street. Jessie loved sewing and worked at Belstaffs

where she became manager of her department.

St Francis Church, Meir Heath, was where Bill and Jessie married and Rev. Bateman was the minister. The church at St Matthews had been subject to subsidence and the colliery had spent money on repairs. Bill informed me it was agreed that another church was needed and at first the land at the top of Windmill Hill, where Mr Barlow lived, was chosen. However, this was not to be and the land belonging to Mr Bailey from Shooters Hills Colour Works was chosen instead. From his home in Sandon Road, Bill could see over Mr Bailey's land and often saw Mr Bailey taking cows from the field to the caves below. Mrs Shatwell lived nearby and had a tennis court by her house, near to where the new church was to be built.

Bill remembers the Home Guard deciding to raise money and build a snooker hall. The clubroom was bought second-hand and the billiard tables bought. As a joiner, Bill made two table-tennis tables for use in the room. Sadly, the hall has been razed to the ground after being so well used and loved for many years by the local people.

When he was an apprentice joiner, Bill was sent to work on a house by Meir Heath water tower. The land belonged to the son of the pottery owner Teddy Brookfield. The firm doing the work was Kettles of Union Street, Longton. Bill was 16 and was at Common Lane putting the roof on to the house.

As he was on the scaffolding, Bill looked towards Shrewsbury and could see a white cloud in the sky. The cloud came nearer and the noise of the engines could be heard as it passed over Common Lane. It was an airship, the R100, and a surprising sight it was.

Bill saw a Zeppelin near to Longton station during the First World War. He was about four years old. There was no blackout then and it came over quite low, following the railway line to Stoke The noise of the diesel engines could be heard and the gondola seen clearly. It dropped bombs at Hanley deep pit but didn't cause much damage, said Bill. The sky was often lit up in that area because they used to smelt iron and the light attracted the Zeppelin, Bill explained with a smile.

When we talked about the windmill, Bill could remember how derelict it was and how it looked with two broken sails. It was dangerous with such rotten wood and so the sails had to be removed to make it safe.

It was interesting to hear that people used to take a radiogram into the windmill tower and have dances. Later on, television was tried there but did not receive very good pictures.

Although Lymers' buses ran from Longton to Meir Heath and to Spot Acre, Bill's family had a car. It was a Morris 12 at first and then he changed it to a Fiat 1100 from Platt's garage. Later, he had a Simca 1000; in fact, four of them. Over the years, Bill recalls how his daughters Linda and Elaine loved to go out in the car.

"What a lovely garden you have." *"That's all down to Howard Platt, my son-in-law,"* said Bill, showing me the conservatory where all the geraniums were potted up, ready to go outside when the chance of frost had gone. There were primulas and polyanthus at present, making a lovely show and a credit to Linda and Howard.

Bill and Jessie enjoyed life together until February 2000 when sadly Jessie passed away aged 87. These photos show when they first went on an aeroplane together.

What a memory William Keeling has. He has invited me to go back again to talk about old times. I thoroughly enjoyed myself and I hope that he did.

W and J Keeling wedding
(By kind permission of W Keeling)

Mr W Keeling at work
(By kind permission of W Keeling)

W and J Keeling going on holiday *(By kind permission of W Keeling)*

W and J Keeling wedding *(By kind permission of W Keeling)*

key-cold   *As cold as a key. A key, on account of the coldness of the metal of which it is composed, was anciently employed to stop any slight bleeding.*

PEOPLE

The Windmill

By Henry Wadsworth Longfellow

By Henry Wadsworth Longfellow
And while we wrestle and strive,
My master, the miller, stands
And feeds me with his hands;
For he knows who makes him thrive,
Who makes him lord of lands

Facts about the Home Guard

Active from 14 May 1940; Country – in United Kingdom; Branch – British Army Role – Defence from invasion; Disbanded – 31 December 1945; Initially Local Defence Volunteers, comprising 1.5 million local volunteers otherwise ineligible for military service, usually owing to age, hence nickname 'Dad's Army'; Britain declared war on Germany, 1 September 1939. Winston Churchill, First Lord of the Admiralty, arranged that some sort of home defence force should be raised. 23 July 1940 – LDV renamed as the Home Guard.

Mr Dudley Holmes

In February 2010, I was featured in an article in the Sentinel newspaper concerning Meir Heath Windmill Project. The following day, Gwyneth Rogers, the daughter of Mr Dudley Holmes, emailed me to say that her father had been in the Home Guard at Meir Heath during World War II because he was unfit for regular service in the forces. That afternoon, Tony and I went to meet Mr Holmes to learn about his time as a Home Guard.

In the summer of 1940, Mr Holmes joined the Local Defence Volunteers (Look Duck Vanish as they were fondly called). These men later became known as the Home Guard after Winston Churchill thought that was a good name for them. Mr Holmes was a volunteer until the very end of the war in 1945.

At the age of 88, Mr Holmes has a very good memory and he told us how the local company was known as E

Company and was based at Cresswell, Stallington, Blythe Bridge and Meir Heath, which was No 21 platoon, E Company, based at the windmill. The Company Commander was Captain E B Shaw with Lieutenant A Wright in charge of 21 Platoon. He left later to become Company Commander and was replaced by W Adams and Lieutenant T G Lawley.

When we talked about the group at the windmill, Mr Holmes said that he did his training duty nights on Tuesday and Thursday for two hours from 7.00pm until 9.00pm and Sunday mornings from 10am to 12 noon. Once every week, he had to do all night duty, 8.00pm until 6.00am the next day.

When on duty, two men would patrol from Meir Heath to Stallington and meet the Home Guard from Stallington. At that time there were no houses in that area, just open fields and woods. The Home Guard would patrol Rough Close and check that area. As the men were aged between 17 and 65+, it was a mixed group, changing all the time because men were taken away by their work or sent into the forces or to do war work.

Mr Holmes painted a picture of the scene in the windmill.

Dudley Holmes – Home Guard
(Photo G Swift)

"Outside there were sandbags round the windmill door, and inside the door a partition divided the ground floor into two sections. On the right-hand side was the office section and on the left of the partition was where we stayed. At the back of the room was a cupboard, and in our section a large ammunition box with a few rounds of ammunition, five rifles and two shotguns. There was a stove pot which created a lot of smoke. When the wind blew, the place was full of smoke and we had to leave the door open so it became very cold." Mr Holmes continued telling us about the huge ladder which stretched up to the top of the tower. *"It was difficult to get up that ladder with army boots on. I had to be very careful not to slip. On the second floor were wooden bunk beds with canvas mattresses."*

Mr Holmes continued:

"On the flat roof of the tower was a small observation turret, into the roof of which was fitted a large iron ring. Attached to the ring was a movable metal sighting tube. It was an ideal watch tower and I could see for miles. I looked for lights showing. On one occasion, the door of the guard room on Meir airfield was left open. I then had the dubious pleasure of contacting Captain Shaw to report this. He was not best pleased since it was after midnight.

After a time, the group decided to raise money for a hut. They obtained an old army hut and put it up, working in their spare time. The building held about 40 people. Later it was taken down to St Francis's Church grounds.

During the war, the government decided to have what was called double summer time and so it stayed light until 11pm at night. The people who didn't like this were the farmers, because it caused dark mornings and was difficult for them."

During his years at Meir Heath as a Home Guard, Mr Holmes remembers the time when The Earl of Harrowby inspected the group. Another occasion was when Area Commander Colonel Evans came for an inspection. He decided that there were to be no more night duties, which pleased the group.

The Home Guard enjoyed the parades they did to raise funds for the war effort. Marchers went to Blythe Bridge Station and other groups, including the American men from Grindley Lane camp, joined the parades.

As a child, Mr Holmes went to Meir junior school and then to the old Longton High. When he left school, he worked at Blythe colour works as a dispatch clerk until 1945. At the end of the war, he decided to train as a teacher and went to study at Alnwick Castle training college on the emergency training programme.

Later, he went to teach at Cheadle County Primary School where he remembers he earned £300 a year and remembers paying 5 pence return for a bus ticket in those days. How times have changed!

Mr Holmes and his wife Mildred (Siddall) had three children: David, Gwyneth and Barbara. At 88, Mr Holmes has a wonderful memory.

Blythe Bridge and Meir Heath Home Guard Platoon 1944

In February 2010, I was featured in an article in the Sentinel newspaper concerning Meir Heath Windmill Project. The following day, Gwyneth Rogers, the daughter of Mr Dudley Holmes, emailed me to say that her father had been in the Home Guard at Meir Heath during World War II because he was unfit for regular service in the forces. That afternoon, Tony and I went to meet Mr Holmes to learn about his time as a Home Guard.

Home Guard

Headquarters: The Windmill

Meir Heath Landlady: Mrs Gimbert (nicknamed The General)

Incumbent St Francis: Father Salter

Overall C/O Major Alf Wright, Barker Bros Potteries

C/O Meir Heath: Lt Lawley, Chemist

Other Ranks

Sgt Bossons: 1914–18 veteran, weapons and drill instructor; Sgt Wilf Oakes: organ builder, transport; Cpl Dave Duddell: Duddell's Brick and Marl, Fenton, dispatch rider; Cpl Sam Oakes: plumber; Eric Dennis: teapot manufacturer; Don Dennis: solicitor, wicket-keeper Longton Cricket Club; Fred Bath: potter of Sherwood Road; Ken Stanier: King's Shropshire Light Infantry; B Stanier: Clive Podmore electric shop, Longton; Ern Bailey: later badly injured in road accident.

Gerard Dean: of Queensmead Road, Royal Marine Commandos, killed in action on D Day, 1944; Ron Ogden: Black Watch, platoon collected for a kilt; Harry Whitfield: North Staffordshire Regt; Bob Hornsall: Commando (Green Berets); Joe Hulse: Quartermaster; Bill Derricott: market gardener; Cyril Tabbener: farm worker; Ernie Bratt; Joe Cliffe; Ben Hill: from London, worked at Rootes aircraft factory; Harold Burton: Royal West African Frontier Force, later Sgt of police, Stoke-on-Trent.

A bacon and egg breakfast later given to both platoons

As most people who live in this area of Meir Heath know, the Home Guard met at the Windmill and the Windmill Inn. The document above had information from Mrs Wilf Oakes and H Burton. Peter Oakes had mentioned that his father, Wilf, was in the Home Guard and it was interesting to see who was there in 1942. Down as organ builder and transport, Wilf Oakes transported the men on the metal sides put onto his trailer. Many people will recognise the name of Dennis, the teapot manufacturer; a very well-known company. All the men remembered came for their turn of duty after a day's work, and looking at the occupations above can be seen a great variety of talent. On the list, the item that made me smile was 'Mrs Gilbert (nicknamed The General)'. That tells us how well thought of she was and how the men enjoyed their connection with the Windmill Inn.

Many thanks to Peter Oakes for all his help.

From 1881 Census Records

Meir Heath People

Here is information from the Fulford Parish Registers collected by the Staffordshire Parish Register Society and transcribed by Andre and Elizabeth Bold. M**ear/Meer Heath = Meir Heath**

'Dusty Miller' Beer House, Meir Heath, Stone, Stafford, England						
	Occuption	Relationship	Marriage	Age	Sex	Birthplace
John Davis	Ag Lab	Head	M	38	M	Montg Wales
Emma Davis		Wife	M	36	F	Welshpool Wales
George Davis	Scholar	Son		10	M	Dudley Stafford Eng
Anne Davis		Dau		8	F	Dudley Stafford Eng
Ellen Davis		Dau		2	F	Milton Stafford Eng
George Walker	Miller	Head	W	42	M	Leek Stafford England
Edwin Walker	Innkeeper	Son	M	21	M	Stone Stafford England
Ursula Walker		Dau-in- law	M	19	F	Norton Stafford England
Hannah Thorley	Dom Serv	Servt	U	40	F	Cheadle Stafford England
William Rushton	Brick Maker	Head	M	26	M	Stone Stafford Eng
Harriet Rushton		Wife	M	24	F	Wolverhampton
John Rushton		Son		11	M	Stone Stafford
William Broome	Ag Lab	Head	W	51	M	Worvely Worcester
Sarah A Broome		Dau	U	17	F	Dowles Shropshire
William Broome	Farm Lab	Son		14	M	Dowles Shropshire
George H Broome	Scholar	Son		11	M	Dowles Shropshire
Elizabeth Broome	Scholar	Dau		8	F	Dalehill Stafford
John Plant	Innkeeper	Head	M	34	M	Longton Stafford
Caroline Plant		Wife	M	35	F	Abbots Bromley Stafford
Elizabeth Plant	Scholar	Dau		11	F	Stone Stafford
Gertrude Plant	Scholar	Dau		9	F	Stone Stafford
Lucy J Plant	Scholar	Dau		8	F	Stone Stafford
William J Plant	Scholar	Son		6	M	Stone Stafford
Florence Plant	Scholar	Dau		3	F	Stone Stafford
Thomas Plant		Son		11wks	M	Stone Stafford
Clara A Smith	Dom Serv	Serv		15	F	Fenton Stafford
John Cheadle	Innkeeper	Head	M	42	M	Stone Stafford
Anne Cheadle		Wife	M	40	F	Cannock Stafford
William Cheadle	Joiner	Son	U	22	M	Stone Stafford
Charles Mear	Ag Lab	Serv	U	45	M	Stone Stafford

Fulford St Nicholas Parish Register

Births	
1813	10th Jan Charles s/o Charles and Eliz Lakin of Bird in Hand, Inn Keeper 19th June Eliz Sarah d/o Richard Clarke and Sarah Hill of Stallington Hall (Gent)
1815	7th Feb Eliz d/o Charles and Dorothy Barrison of Black Lake, Gamekeeper 17th Benjamin s/o Benjamin Hannah Hilton of Blacklake, Innkeeper 22nd June Mary d/o David and Mary Copeland of Gravelly Bank, Innkeeper 18th Aug Robert s/o Robert and Ann Fairbanks of Bird in Hand, Weaver 7th Sept Helen d/o Will and Helen Wilshaw of Black Lake, Horse braker
1816	26th Sept Will John Jackson s/o Sarah Amery Windmill, Farmer
1817	14th Jan Eliz d/o Daniel and Mary Copeland of Gravelly Bank, Publican
1820	30th Jan Thomas s/o William and Sarah Emery of Windmill, Farmer
1822	1st March Louise d/o Peter and Ann Gregory of Fulford, Millwright
1826	2nd April John s/o Rich and Mary Wheal of Windmill, Victualler 11th June Sarah d/o Charles and Hannah Swift of Meer Heath, Iron Moulder
1829	22nd Feb Ann dau of Joseph and Hannah Snipe of Windmill Common
1834	28th Dec Jane d/o Joseph and Mary Bridgwood of Gravelly Bank, Labourer

Fulford Register

Burials				
1813	7th Feb	William Hough	Hilderstone	10 yrs
	21st May	Ann Barker	Fulford	87 yrs
	14th Sept	Charles Adams	Rough Close	1 month
1816	9th Jan	Mary Ash	Fulford	6 yrs
	15th May	William Cotton		infant
	11th Aug	Thomas Ash	Stallington	2 yrs
	8th Dec	Samuel Fenton	Fulford	5 months
1817	27th Jan	Joseph Crowther	Stallington Grange	19 yrs
1819	4th June	David Tansley	Leaden Dale	9 weeks
1820	18th Aug	Mary Ash	Windmill	70 yrs
	21st Dec	Rev Wilm Lindley Wragg	per Curate Fulford Hall	29 yrs
1833	11th May	Mary Copeland	Gravelly Bank	46 yrs
1835	6th Apr	The Reverend John Dunderdale	Fulford Hall	33 yrs
	14th Apr	Wm Fenton	Gravelly Bank	51 yrs
1825	23rd Jan	Wm Rogers	Meer Heath	3 yrs
1827	28th Nov	Mary Oakes	Windmill	80 yrs
1831	1st June	Wm Aimison	Mear Heath	7 weeks
1835	31st Jan	Eliz Finney	Mear Heath	67 yrs
	15th Nov	George Hastings	Windmill Common	46 yrs
	7th Apr	Ann Hasketh	Windmill Common	20 yrs
	25th Apr	John Chesworth	Mear	7 yrs
	17th July	Ann Chesworth	Mear Heath	35 yrs
	13th Oct	Thomas Broster	Blythe Marsh	67 yrs

Events

The audience

Lewis Roberts and Jack Emery dress for the occasion

A Mitchell-Waite entertains the visitors with
Laurel and Hardy Film Show

C Latham – Sweet Melody Dreamboat Band at The Crown Hotel, Longton

J Unwin, M Sturgess, B Lockett and C Gunn at an event at Heron Cross Club

Nita and Clive Mould at the Sweet Melody Dream Boat Band at Heron Cross Senior Citizens Club
– Money raised for the Windmill Fund (2009) *(Photo G Swift)*

(Photo G Swift)

Enjoying the tea at Mary Queen Scots Evening – Mr and Mrs Humphries, Mrs Colclough, Mrs Bell

L Smith as Mary Queen of Scots at Rough Close & Meir
Heath Village Hall – a wonderful talk enjoyed by all

Mrs Walker, J Walker and A Evans

Brenda Smith and Peter Lawton with Mr and Mrs Bell at the Fish Supper

Christmas Carol Concert at Lightwood
Methodist Church to raise money for the project – Dr M Salt, D Middleton, James Pointon and Naomi Salt *(Photo G Swift)*

Nic Hawkins talks about seafood (Seafresh.co.uk) with June and Tony Lane, Kath Nixon and Muriel Warrilow

Windmill Wacky Races held at Florence Sports and Social Club (2009) – D Bestwick, A Swift and S Beardmore
(Photo G Swift)

Blythe Bridge Rotary Club meets at the Upper House, Barlaston, and Sam Lanza invited the Chairman to talk about the Windmill Project; the members gave a donation to Mr Swift for the fund

M Upton presenting B Smith with the prize at the quiz evening

J Upton and S Clare score keeping at the quiz

S Clare

At the Music Hall – E and B Sale with C and J Slater *(Photo G Swift)*

Ladies at the Music Hall evening

£2. 50

Please bring this Catalogue with you.

ROUGH CLOSE FARM

ROUGH CLOSE

On the Main Longton to Stone and Stafford Road.
A frequent Bus Service runs past the farm.

W. S. BAGSHAW & SONS

Have received instructions fron Mr. W. MASON (who is
forming an Attested Herd) to sell by auction,
entirely without reserve, on—

THURSDAY, SEPTEMBER 30TH, 1954

His Valuable Farming Stock, comprising—

32 HEAD OF COMMERCIAL Friesians

Viz—An Exceedingly Grand Dairy Herd of 25 Young
Cows and Heifers; Capital Hereford Stock Bull; 4
Yearling Heifers; and 2 Young Hereford Cross Heifer
Calves

8 Feeding Pigs   50 Caponized Cockerels

SALE at ONE o'clock

Auction & Valuation Offices—Uttoxeter, Ashbourne, Bakewell, Derby

F. A. HARPER, PRINTER, UTTOXETER.

John Mason – Water Bailiff

J Mason *(Photo A Swift)*

Mason family wedding

**The Mason Family
– John, Robert, Rosemarie, David, Alan and George Mason**

Showing room in mill ready for a meeting (Available for hire)

Mason family wedding

The Auctioneers have no hesitation in calling the attention of all Agriculturalists to this important Sale. The Dairy Cows are a very good lot, mostly of Friesian type, and as 22 of them are due to calve during the autumn a very good opportunity is afforded to winter milk producers of acquiring some really excellent milkers. The Hereford Stock Bull is a grand animal and fit to join any herd.

(By kind permission of J Mason)

John Mason Talking about the Farm in the Pottery Accent

Glossary

To help with the understanding of this local North Staffs dialect, this glossary shows a translation of some of the words used in the interview with Mr J Mason. This dialect is part of our heritage and we hope that it never disappears from our area.

abite	*about*	noss	*nurse*
afe	*half*	owd	*old*
ah	*I*	owees	*always*
atner	*aren't*	paise	*piece*
awee	*away*	peen	*paying*
bate	*beat*	raight	*right*
befoer	*before*	rind	*round*
betwain	*between*	sane	*seen*
bin	*been*	ser	*so*
brine	*brown*	shape	*sheep*
brokken	*broken*	snappin	*food*
brote	*brought*	stoo	*stool*
chase	*cheese*	tack	*take*
cnna	*can't*	taters	*potatoes*
compo	*compensation*	thase	*these*
cosna	*can't you*	thay	*thay*
cudst	*could you*	toke	*talk*
dine	*down*	towd	*told*
djed	*dead*	towkin	*talking*
dust	*do you*	tray	*tree*
fer	*for*	unna	*is not*

fo	*fall*	waiter	*water*
foer	*four*	way've	*we have*
grind	*ground*	weet	*wait*
lark	*like*	weh	*we*
mac	*make*	weshin	*washing*
mard	*cry baby*	wick	*week*
marn	*mine*	wom	*home*
munner	*must not*	wona	*will not*
nah	*no*	yed	*head*
naight	*night*		

When I bought the document showing the sale at the farm, I guessed that it was John's father's farm at Rough Close and I thought how interesting it was and if I could ask John more about it. Leaving a note through his cottage door, I was pleased when he rang and arranged to meet Tony and I to talk about the document and his father's farm.

Here is his talk in the Pottery dialect!

Mayan Ma Friend Jack Revisited!

John says:

"Adoo Gill. Its greet te say they agin."

Gill:

"I'm very pleased to see you John."

John:

"That theer document wuz me faythers ferm, Rough Close ferm. A wuz a booy them days.

A wuz bun in Roz cottage. May brothuz Robert James, Alan Albert, Davis Lesley, Oliver George and are sista Rosemarie Hilda.

Way ow livd on th ferm with fayther an maytha. John William wuz knarn uz Billy.

Nah at worn in 1954, me fayther browt cayn te av sum cattle. Theese wuz TT tested te replace otha cattle.

Me fayther wuz nown fe advice ay wud giv abyt hosesn cattle.

A ad thus herd an deceeded best te av urn TT testd.

Ar went we im an John Payma te Otley in Yorkshire an way went fe new cows.

A wuz fiftayne un sat in th front cab uv cattle truck.

Way ad 23 milkers, rest wuz heffers. Brayd wuz frieziens nah thee called Holstens.

That teer catalogue is th ferm sale.

Ferm wuz 70 acres and laita me fayther ad nother 30 acres so e ad 100 acres o te gether.

Ar faylds. Near ferm ad name.

Wun wuz the Craft, the meadow, cattle went e theer afta milkin. Grind ontother sayd o main road wer 15 acre Berry

Hill fayld, the 6 acrs bottom fayl dw to bonks and Naggies lane.

Cupple pools across theer.

Ar luv et up theer. Badgers and foxes play."

What a memory John has! We talked about when he went, aged 15, with his father Billy Mason to the markets at Newcastle and Uttoxeter. Having no car, they travelled by double-decker bus, going through Stramshall to Uttoxeter. When it was the County Show, Mr Mason took cattle to the showground. Here is a photograph of Alan Mason and Rosemarie Mason with the prize-winning cow, Stoneroad Gem. They were delighted that the animal won first prize. It was a cow they had bred on the farm. Another cow at the show was Brockton Huntsmere 17th. This cow was known for the milk it produced after calving, sometimes as much as 12 gallons a day.

Over the years, John enjoyed fishing and became the Water Bailiff, 1994, of the Bibby's Angling Club. He says it is the best club in Stoke-on-Trent and for 18 years he has looked after the pools at Rough Close.

John enjoyed fishing in his father's pool and carried on in 1991 when Tim Evans bought the farm and together they organised digging out other pools. It was then that they allowed Bibby's Angling Club to rent the pools in about 1994. All the pools have names.

R Mason and A Mason

The football team

The football team

The photograph is of John when he played football for Meir Heath FC. They used Meir airfield for a pitch. When the team started, the first meetings were held in a barn at the farm.

I have been interested in the big house on Windmill Hill. Now it is Windmill Hill Children's Nursery. While he was visiting us, John talked about this house, which was Tommy Degg's house. It was on the hill going to the top, on the right-hand side and near to Rough Close Farm. John said that he had worked as a joiner there.

Thomas Degg, or Tommy as he was known, owned race horses. He kept stables in Hartwell Lane – the lane leading to Barlaston. John was lucky, following tips he received from the Degg household. He remembered a horse called Trentham Boy, a fine horse trained by Jack Gosden, winning the November handicap at Manchester.

Married to Dawn, John has sons Peter David, and Paul John William. He is the proud grandfather of Dawn Louise, who is nearly 16 months old, and he can't wait until she is old enough to be taken fishing. Tony and I enjoyed our afternoon talking about old times with John Mason who has wonderful memories.

Local Businesses

Windmill Hill Day Nursery

After talking to John Mason about Tommy Degg's house on Windmill Hill, I decided to go and have a look. I was met at this imposing building by Samantha Brian (Blackburn). She made me feel really welcome and rang her dad, Graham Blackburn, to ask him to check dates for me. The information I was after was when the house had been built by Thomas Degg. Samantha's dad said that it had been built in 1958. At that time, Tom Degg had a stud farm in Hartwell Lane. In the house is a beautiful window, showing a love of horses. After the Degg family lived there, the house was sold to Mr and Mrs Whalley and then in 1985, Mr and Mrs Graham Blackburn bought the house. It became a nursery and still is, with Samantha and husband Scott in charge. It is a lovely place for children. A happy atmosphere as children and nurses were seen in the house and gardens. Samantha said:

"Welcome to Windmill Hill Private Day Nursery… Our nursery is a family-run business which was established in 1984 and is set in 7 acres of land in the rural countryside area of Rough Close; from 1984, the nursery occupied the ground floor of the building and in 2005 was renovated and developed to occupy both the ground and first floor of the building. Full-time and part-time care provision is available for children aged from 3 months to 5 years, including school run and school club."

Mr K – the Dentist

John Kocierz BDS

There is nothing worse than toothache. Everybody knows that! "Open Wide."

However, if you are fortunate enough to be a patient at Meir Heath Dental Surgery, life is made easier because you have: John Kocierz BDS, Jayne Hugh BDS, Lyn Kocierz, Christine Stanier, Julie Fawkes, Stephanie Morris, Clara Littler, Vickie Tooth and Alison Peobles. They are the team.

Whenever you ring up, they are always there to help and find you an appointment quickly. Situated at 404 Sandon Road, Meir Heath, a car park at the front of the building leads you into a pleasant waiting room. In there, music plays softly in the background and there are magazines available to read. As I wait for my turn, I think of Pam Ayres' poem, 'I wish I'd looked after my teeth!' As you enter the rooms, you are always met by either Lyn Kocierz or one of the receptionists with a smile and a friendly word or two. You start to relax straight away. One of the dental nurses comes to fetch you and takes you into the surgery where John Kocierz greets you cheerfully and reassures you straight away. You know that you are in safe hands. John always has lovely, very colourful ties and I expect the children who visit are pleased to see them. As you sit in the surgery, you can see the well-kept garden through the window and, of course, the surgery has all the latest equipment.

John has had the practice for 21 years and is well known in the area. He trained at Birmingham University Dental School and met his wife Lyn at Coventry when they were both working. They have three children: Laura, who is a Doctor in Birmingham (IThs Anaesthetics); Jim, who is at PricewaterhouseCoopers in Birmingham after serving with the paras; and Rich, who is at Liverpool University Dental School.

John and Lyn bought the property in August 1990. The semi had John's mum in the other half of the building and the surgery opened in January 1991. They provided National Health Service treatment to the patients. In 2005, Ann Marie Howells joined them as a dentist until 2005. In 2009, Jayne Hughes BDS joined the team. Christine Stanier joined in 1991 and Julie Fawkes in 1998, with Stephanie Morris joining in 2002. John and all the team have supported the Windmill Project, and Meir Heath Preservation Group thanks them for their help.

Deryn Reynolds

Everyone has a lovely time when they go to Deryn's. Yes, if you go to Deryn's salon, Hilderstone Road, Meir Heath, you will enjoy your visit. As well as having your hair done, you can have a cup of coffee and a friendly chat. Deryn trained at Hulses' hairdressers in Newcastle after leaving school. "Where have 40 years gone?" Deryn said when I called to see her, Annette Pettitt and Cathy Willock. Megan Poole is the Saturday girl. Annette has worked there for 34 years and Cathy for 20 years, so they make a very good team. It's a traditional hairdressers and one that is popular in Meir Heath.

The window showing the racehorses in what had been
Mr T Degg's house on Windmill Hill

Samantha Brian at the Windmill Day Nursery *(Photo G Swift)*

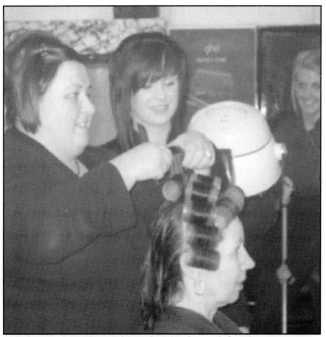

S Lacono, L Deakin and S Anderson who work for Theo Georgiou
(Photo G Swift)

Peter Oakes

Mr and Mrs K Moore, Meir Heath Post Office and Stores

On 8 August 2008, Kashir and Daljit Moore moved into Rough Close Post Office with their children: Kiren, Ravi and Sharan. As well as the Post Office, they run the Premier Shop, which is very well stocked. One of the items found there are the lovely Box Lane oatcakes.

Theo Georgiou

International Hair Design,
Beauty Therapy and Sunbeds.
T: 01782 317521, Grindley Lane, Meir Heath.
Stylists: Stacy Lacono, Lawri Deakin, and Sarah Anderson.

Little Acorn – John Oakes and Son, Organ Builder

John Oakes was married to Jesse and first lived in Fenton at the business, which was also a drapers shop. In April 1926, they decided to move to Hilderstone Road; Meir Heath. They did this because Jesse had been ill and wanted to live in a bungalow. After all these years, this family business is still in Hilderstone Road.

Peter Oakes told us about John, his grandfather, and Wilfred, his father, who had both worked building pipe organs. Wilfred was married to Doris. They had a daughter Margaret and a son Peter. Peter Oakes is married to Ruth and they have a daughter Linda and son Michael.

John had been a miner but decided to work on reed organs and, later, pipe organs. Wilfred joined him in the business in 1922 and their apprentice was Tony Johnson, who joined them in 1931 (age 14). Wilf took over the business in 1954 after John died at the age of 80, and he was in charge until 1980. In 1973, Peter joined the family business and, as we realise next year is 2013, the business will be into its centenary year. When we talked about the building of organs, Peter told us:

"The pipes can be made from lead/tin alloy or zinc and even, rarely, copper. Wooden pipes are used and produce a more muffled sound. Organs usually have 61 notes at the maximum. The effective length of pipes can be altered by moving a flap or extra tuning slide or stopper to tune the organ. The lead pipes usually give a deeper resonant sound. A wind supply was needed – years ago, a boy would hand-blow by using a lever or crank wheel operating the feeders-bellows (wind reservoir) and the pressure provided by this wind blows the organ."

As Peter explained, this was in the years before mains electricity.

After WW1 and electricity was available, Wilf and John decided they needed to improve the old system, which was very noisy. They developed a blower motor. This was encased and blew a fair volume of air. In Stoke-on-Trent, these blowers were fitted to organs and Wilf developed his own line in blowers.

They were successful and John needed a name for it. His wife, Jesse, said, *"Let's call it Acorn Blower; after all, we are Oakes."* That's how the machine received its name. Peter showed us photographs of organs that they had built. It was interesting to hear of a very special organ made after instructions from Rev. Edgar Bland. This organ had to be crated up by Wilf (180 pipes) and sent to St Georges Church, Gingerland, Nevis and West Indies. In 1974, the organ as sent to Edgar Bland was, as it happened, the last organ made on site to date.

It was interesting to hear how special this organ was. Wilf realised that in the West Indies wood termites were a problem. The iron frame worked on by Les Moore was started in 1967. It wasn't until 1973 that the organ was finished. This was quite a long time. Usually an organ could be made in about six months.

Mr & Mrs Oakes

J Oakes, W Oakes, T Johnson Hollins, K Kane and L Moore

The Organ

Adverts from St Francis Parish Magazine (1966)

In 1953, the organ for Carmount Crematorium was completed in six months and the one at St Francis Church, Meir Heath, was made in this usual time, although some delay was due to its completion after the start of WWII.

Peter Oakes still spends part of his working week seeing to organs that need tuning or rebuilding, or need maintenance work doing, and the rest of the time on office work or other work. He is proud that his family have been working on organs for nearly a hundred years and that many of the organs that produced such beautiful music were made or rebuilt by the company at Meir Heath.

Local Businesses

1876: Kelly's Directory of Staffordshire			
Bailey (Mrs)	*Shooter's Hill*	**John Bailey**	*Colour Manufacturer, Shooter's Hill*
Charles Benbow	*Farmer*	**William Bentley**	*Assistant Overseer*
William Bloor	*Farmer, Lightwood Farm*	**John Brassington**	*Swynnerton Arms and Farmer*
Benjamin Brooks	*Farmer, Hartwell*	**James Brooks**	*Shopkeeper and Timber Merchant*
William Brooks	*Farmer*	**William Brooks Jnr**	*Farmer and Timber Merchant*
John Cheadle	*Butcher*	**John Cheadle**	*Grocer*
James Dawson	*Wheelwright*	**Thomas Goodwin**	*Blacksmith*
John Hall	*Miller & Beer Retailer*	**George Hand**	*George and Dragon*
George Heapy	*Windmill Inn*	**Joseph Hodgkinson**	*Farmer*
Daniel Lowe	*Farmer*	**John Myatt**	*Farmer, Berry Hill*
Jabez Smith	*Beer Retailer, Shooter's Hill*	**Thomas Smith**	*Farmer*
William Taylor	*Silk Lawn Manufacturer*	**Chas Thomas**	*Farmer, Lightwood Lodge*
Thomas Wooley	*Beer Retailer & Butcher, Shooters Hill*	**George Wooliscroft**	*Butcher*
Hannah Bridgewood	*Shopkeeper*	**Jason Brooks & Sons – Timber Merchants (English)**	
Thomas Brooks	*Shopkeeper, Post Office*	**James Cliffe**	*George and Dragon*
James Dawson	*Swynnerton Arms & Wheelwright*	**George Goodwin**	*Blacksmith*
Henry Latham	*Cowkeeper*		

1904: Kelly's Directory of Staffordshire			
Arthur Bailey	*Shooter's Hill*	**Alfred Emerkeil**	*Villa Godesberg*
William Henry	*Malkin*	**James Smith**	*Springcroft*
Henry Thorley	*Hay & Straw Dealer*	**Edwin A Turner**	*Farmer*
George Wooliscroft	*Butcher*		

1924: Kelly's Directory of Staffordshire			
Arthur Bailey	*Shooter's Hill*	**Harold Bott**	*Lorraine*
Hamlet P Embrey	*Lyndhurst*	**Ernest Hawley**	*Dean Lodge*
Leeson (Mrs)	*Arnold Villa*	**Arthur Bailey**	*Colour Manufacturer, Shooter's Hill*
Charles Bedson	*Milk Seller, Dale House, Leadendale*	**Charles Benbow**	*Farmer, Wood End Farm*
Thomas Brian	*Cowkeeper*	**John Day**	*Blacksmith*
John Deakin	*Wheelwright*	**Joseph Embrey**	*Farmer*
William Hughes	*Swynnerton Arms*	**Colin Stephen James**	*George and Dragon*
A M Key (Mrs)	*Shopkeeper, Post Office*	**Harold Shelley**	*Farmer, Cophurst*
Charles Turner	*Farmer*	**Lydia Williams (Mrs)**	*Grocer*
George Wooliscroft	*Butcher*		

1924: Meir Heath:			
Mrs Charles Benbow	*Highcroft*	**John Pepper**	*Leadendale House*
William Fenton	*Farmer*	**Alfred Ernest Gimbert**	*Windmill Inn*
Joseph Taylor	*Cowkeeper*		

1932: Meir Heath:			
Alfred Joseph Austin	*Shopkeeper*	**Sydney H Barlow**	*Highcroft*
Jas Bullock	*Shopkeeper*	**Chas R Challinor**	*Smallholder, The Hollies*
Alfred Ernest Gimbert	*Windmill Inn*	**Arthur Liversage**	*Shopkeeper*
Harriet Gertrude Nixon (Mrs)	*Newsagent*	**J Oakes & Sons**	*Organ Builders*
John Pepper	*Leadendale House*	**George Ratcliffe**	*Boot Repairer*
Robinson Jnr	*Farmer, The Poplars*	**William Tewksbury**	*Petrol Station*
William Warrilow	*Poultry Farmer*		

With thanks to E Hallam for researching this section.

1785 – The Will of Elizabeth Walklate, Meir Heath

This is the last Will and Testament of Elizabeth Walklate of Meir Heath in the Parish of Stoke-upon-Trent in the County of Staffordshire. Follows, concerning all that my Dwelling House standing and being on Meer Heath wherein I now dwell together Garden and all the singular Appurtenance thereunto belonging, I hereby give and devise the same unto my Daughter Margaret Cooper and her heirs forever. I likewise give and devise unto my Daughter Sarah Jarvis and Eleanor Gallimore and my Grandaughter Sarah Gallimore and all that my Croft and piece of Land nearby adjoining to my said Dwelling House subject never the less to the Payment of all my just Debts of what nature and or kind so ever. Which my mind it shall be paid By my said Daughter Sarah Jarvis and Eleanor Gallimore and my GrandDaughter Sarah Gallimore in equal portions and from and after Payment of all such Debts them I devise the said Croft unto the said Sarah Jarvis and Eleanore Gallimore and Sarah Gallimore to be equally be divided among them share and share alike.

Likewise give and bequeath unto my said Grandaughter Sarah Gallimore one half of all my pewter, one Bed Bolster, and two Blankets, an Oak Chest and one Deal box to be delivered one year after my Decease and for that rest residue and all remainder of my goods household goods I give and bequeath the same unto my said Daughter Margaret Cooper and my mind further is that what I have given unto my said Daughter Margaret Cooper shall be to her own private and separate use without the control or intermeddling of her husband Richard Cooper or any other husband with whom she may happen to marry.

I nominate constitute and appoint my said Daughter Margaret Cooper sole Executrix of this my Last will and Testament revoking all wills by me at any time made.

In Witness whereof I have set my Hand and Seal 20th day of March in the year of our Lord one thousand and seven hundred and eighty five signed, sealed, published and declared by the above named Margaret Walklate to be her last will and Testament in the presence of us who have here unto subscribed our Names and Witness in the presence of the Testatrix. And in the presence of each other.

Thomas Harding
the mark of Elizabeth Walklate
Samuel Hartley   X
SEAL O
The mark of Mary Plant X

This will is very interesting and makes us wonder why Elizabeth Walklate didn't like Richard Cooper, her daughter's husband. A bed was a main piece of furniture. Beds were not as we know them now. The base of the bed was a rectangular frame with ropes stretched across in a latticework. On top of this was a crude mattress filled with straw. This was known as a bolster. We now have an expression 'sleep tight; watch the bed bugs don't bite!' This expression relates to the ropes and insects in the straw bolster. This is about the time of King George III.

When I found the will of Margaret Walklate, I was interested because she came from Meir Heath and thought it would also be interesting to see if any of her descendants could be found. I emailed Celia Shemilt, who can usually find details on the internet and has helped me before. Celia rang me, having found that Margaret Walklate's granddaughter, Sarah Gallimore, had married Josiah Beck in Dilhorne Church on 23 January 1787. Sarah's mother, Eleanor, was married to Nicholas Gallimore, and they were married on 29 March 1765, again at Dilhorne Church.

Josiah Beck was the son of James and Mary Beck from the parish of Caverswall.

Another friend who helps in searching is Eileen Hallam. She sent me this information and I am grateful to her for the help she gave and how quickly it arrived

Information Relating to Elizabeth Walklate

Sarah Gallimore, born 1775, married John Aynsley senior (1752–1829), grandfather of THE John Aynsley. John owned property at Gallimore's Bank (Longton Precinct). I think this was Sarah's mother, Jane, and she was married in 1777. There is a tree on familysearch.org, which has a Sarah Gallimore bapt. 5 Sept 1765, Dilhorne, parents Ralph and Eleanor. She married Josiah Beck in 1787 at Dilhorne. Eileen goes on to say: "However, there is a note on the IGI as daughter of Ralph and Elizabeth. I have listed her as daughter of Ralph and Eleanor because he was the only Ralph having children in Dilhorne at that time. It is possible that Elizabeth was the first wife and Eleanor the second wife." I wonder why Elizabeth Walklate didn't want her son-in-law to get any of her possessions.

Information from Fulford Parish Register

Births		
1816	26th Sept	William John Jackson, son of William and Sarah Amery. Windmill. Farmer
1818	6th Feb	Richard Ash, son of William and Sarah Amery of Windmill.
1820	31st Jan	Thomas, s of William and Sarah Emery, Windmill, farmer.
1822	1st March	Louisa, d of Peter and Ann Gregory of Fulford, Millwright.
1822	7th July	Charlotte, d of John and Ann Warrilow, Windmill, labourer.
1823	29th June	William, s of Peter and Ann Gregory, Hilderstone, Millwright.
1824	7th Feb	Eliz, d of Eliza & Matthew Talbot of Normacot, Gate Keeper of the Turnpike.
1825	June	Harriott, d of Peter and Ann Gregory, Hilderstone, Millwright.
1826	2nd April	John, s of Rich and Mary Wheat of Windmill, victualler.
1826	11th June	Sarah, d of Charles and Hannah Swift of Mear Heath, Iron moulder.
1829	22nd Feb	Ann, d of Joseph and Hannah Snape of Windmill, Common Lab.
1834	21st March	Adam and Ann Malkin of Moddershall, Miller.
1836	27th March	John Shenton, son of Mary Ash, Wund Mill Common, servant spinster.
1836	13th Nov	Edward, s of Edward and Catherine Rushton of Wind Mill Common

Burials				
1817	2nd June	Thomas Burton	42	Windmill
	19th Nov	Eliz Plant	71	(Signed Margaret Walklate's Will 1785)
1820	18th Aug	Mary Ash	70	Windmill
1826	4th June	Michael Hall	79	Windmill Common
1827	28th Nov	Mary Oakes	80	Windmill
1835	15th Nov	George Hastings	80	Windmill Common
1836	7th April	Ann Heskith	20	Windmill Common

Meir Heath.

LOT 535.

A very desirable

SMALL HOLDING

situate at Meir Heath, and possessing frontage to the Main Road leading from Leek to Stafford. This Lot consists of

Roomy and substantially built Dwelling House, Out-Offices, Out-Buildings, together with several Crofts of excellent Old Turf, the whole having an Area of 6A. OR. 16P.

THE HOUSE—brick built and tiled—contains Entrance Lobby, Kitchen, Scullery, Dairy, and Two Bedrooms.

Wash House and E. C.

The Out Buildings—brick built and tiled, excepting where otherwise stated—consist o Cow House, with tying for 4, and with Lofting over; Cart Shed, Pig Box, and timbe built and tiled Poultry House.

Tenant:—MR. JAMES SMITH.

Present Apportioned Yearly Rent £13 1s. 0d.

| Outgoings:—Land Tax | ... | 6s. 6d. |
| Water Rate | ... | 9s. 8d. |

he Timber on the land has been measured up, and valued at controlled price of £5.

Notice to quit has been given, which will expire with 25th March, 1920.

SCHEDULE.

ish of Fulford.

O. ON PLAN.	DESCRIPTION.				AREA. ACRES.	AREA. A. R. P.
64	House, Garden, Pasture, etc.			...	1.406	
66	Pasture	...	...	...	1.889	
67	Ditto	...	...	...	1.132	
68	Ditto	...	...	...	1.671	
					6.098	6 0 16

Black Lake Farm, Meir Heath, Duke of Sutherland's Sale (1919)

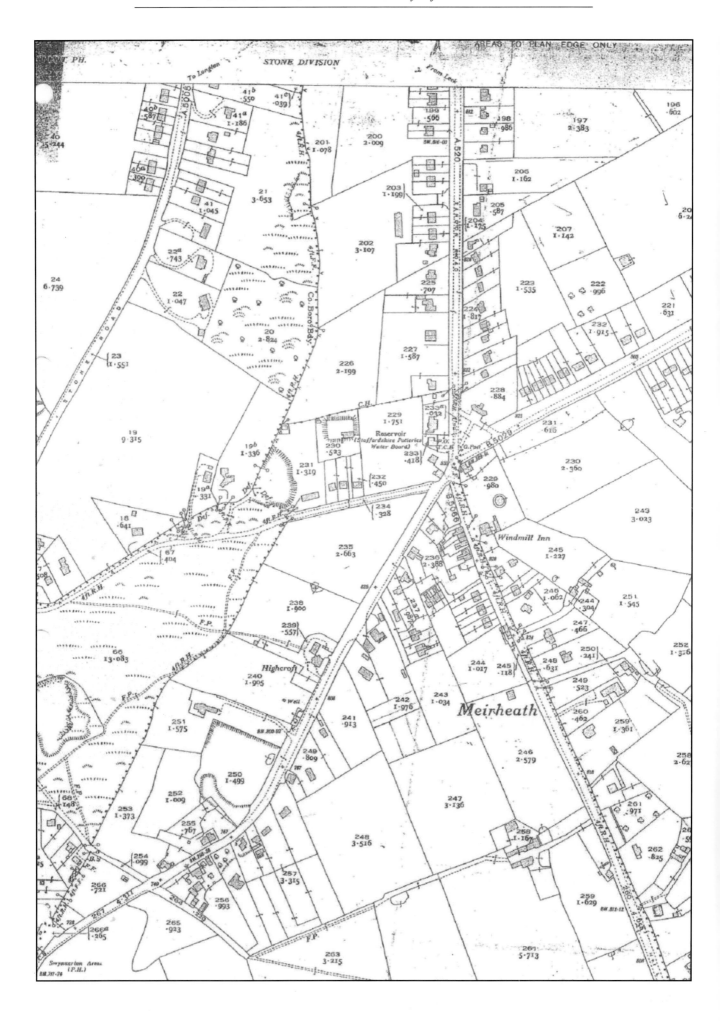

Map of Meir Heath showing the Five Ways

curing-drops *The last drops of medicine in a glass.*

TRY, TRY AGAIN!

The Windmill

By Henry Wadsworth Longfellow

On Sundays I take my rest;
Church-going bells begin
Their low, melodious din;
I cross my arms on my breast,
And all is peace within.

Applying for a Lottery Grant (2010)

The Secretary put together the bid for a grant and this took approximately four weeks to do – so much collecting of requested information.

The Chairman and Secretary/Project Manager went to meet Liz Shaw at the Lord Longford Inn, Cannock.

On the preliminary questionnaire for the lottery grant, it asked if the group had a lease, but nothing about breaks in the lease. This now meant that Phase 2 had to be put on hold, in May 2009. After passing the first stage, where it asked if the group had a lease and Articles of Association etc., the Secretary was sent the next set of forms for the grant. A phone call from the lottery lady, Liz Shaw, said that so far the forms were correct, but that she would like to meet the Chairman and Secretary at Cannock. When the Chairman and Secretary went to meet Mrs Shaw at Cannock, she suggested extra items to include in the bid. One was a bibliography of all the Committee, explaining their occupations and interests. Another idea was to encourage a local Duke of Edinburgh group to volunteer to work with us. She also thought that interviews on video with older members of the community, saving their memories, would help the application, and a list of all the events the group had organised in the past year. The Secretary went away and started to collect the information asked for. When the second meeting was arranged, Laura McDonald from Stafford District Voluntary Services went with the Chairman and Secretary to take notes of the meeting.

At the meeting, a man called Mark Humphries was present and he said that it was necessary for their legal team to

see the full lease. They knew from the first application forms that we had a 25-year lease at peppercorn rent or we could not have been passed to stage 2.

The Secretary gave him the lease and everyone went away. Our hopes of a grant were raised because all the details asked for had been supplied. Two days after this, Liz Shaw rang the Secretary to say the Heritage Lottery would not give a grant or part of a grant because there are five-year breaks in the lease, which mean the group can give back the mill to the M&B company or the M&B Company can claim the windmill tower back.

What a disappointment after all that work collecting the information! The Committee was devastated after hearing that news.

Showing part of the rotten woodwork from the top floor – no nails or screws used, just pegs in holes

The SBC Officer kindly wrote to Mrs Shaw to support our application.

Letter from Stafford Borough Conservation (SBC) Officer Penny McKnight to Liz Shaw (24 June 2010)

Dear Ms Shaw

REPAIR AND RESTORATION WORKS AT MEIR HEATH WINDMILL

I write in support of the application for Heritage Lottery Fund grant by the Meir Heath Windmill Preservation Group.

The Friends have Listed Building Consent for the works to date, and for the proposed rendering works. The scheme combines essential repairs, a degree of reinstatement, and some minor alterations, such as fully glazing a door opening, to facilitate active use of the building as a local heritage resource. The works carried out to date include windows accurately reproducing late-19th century joinery, lime wash to the first-floor interior walls, replacement of the principal timbers for the dust floor, and reproduction of the boat cap. Replacement loft ladders give practical access to the first and second floors, which are not anticipated to be for public access in the near future.

The boat cap has been designed to give a near-accurate external appearance of the historic structure, to enhance the visual and interpretative values of the listed building, but without being a structurally precise reconstruction. Given the aims and budget of the Preservation Group, it was considered unnecessarily onerous to require a fully operational cap, capable of turning and taking sails.

The Meir Heath Windmill was previously on the Stafford Borough Council register of listed buildings at risk, due to a leaking roof, rotten internal timbers and cementitious pointing carried out by the previous owner. The works are fully supported, not only for addressing these essential repairs and taking the building 'out of risk', but also as positively enhancing the special historic and architectural interest of the building through further reinstatement, and creating an appropriate active use for the building. I am happy to see that the works to date have been carried out to a high standard.

The elements of reinstatement have largely been based on photographic evidence from the late 19th century. This includes evidence that the windmill was formerly either whitewashed or rendered. It is hoped that the render will also address issues of dampness in the building as well as protecting the existing brickwork. The building has not yet had an opportunity to fully dry out. However, the external walls have been repointed in a cement-rich mortar and the interior of the first floor of the building was lined with concrete to the first floor for its mid-20th century use as a water tank. The natural breathability of the masonry is therefore threatened. A lime render should act as a sacrificial layer bridging the cement mortar and allowing natural evaporation from the building.

The proposals also include for a drainage channel to be constructed around the base of the mill, to insure against ground-up saturation of the walls.

The proposal therefore has the full support of the Stafford Borough Conservation Officer, as both reinstating a historic finish, and protecting the condition of the building.

Meir Heath Primary School

The school is situated in Golborn Drive, Meir Heath. When it opened in 1967, the first head teacher was Miss A Fisher, who stayed there until 23 April 1990. Mr R Williams was the next head teacher and was appointed on 24 April 1990 to 31 October 1994. Following Mr Williams was Mr P Siddley, 1 November 1994 to 31 August 2010. The present head teacher is Mrs J Luke.

When Miss Fisher was head teacher, she thought it would be a good idea if the children had a logo on their T-shirts. She asked the parents and they thought it sensible to have a competition and to let the children design the logo. Many designs were considered before one was finally chosen.

Sandon High School, Now Sandon Business and Enterprise College

In March 2009, I wrote to Miss Barbara Hall, the head teacher of Sandon High School. As ever, Miss Hall was very helpful and willing to support the Windmill Project.

These letters explain what she offered.

More Supporters

When we had the Laurel and Hardy film shows at The Crown Hotel, Longton, we were pleased when Mary came with helpers and residents from Eldon House. They all enjoyed the visit. The next time they joined us was for the concert at Heron Cross Club, entertained by the Stoneage Singers. Mary and the ladies all enjoyed singing the old favourites.

The U3A Group, the Stoneagers, came to Heron Cross Senior Citizen's Club to sing a selection of songs. This was at the kind invitation of June and Tony Lane, the club leaders. Everyone enjoyed the old songs with tea and biscuits afterwards, and the Windmill Group was pleased to accept a donation towards the Windmill Project.

At a committee meeting, John Bradbeer was volunteered to make a large wooden thermometer appealing for funds. It was thought that the community might give donations to the project. Also at this time the group had a noticeboard made, on which was information about the mill. Helen Johnson, Development Officer, Shugborough Museum Grant Department and Trustees, granted the group the money for the noticeboard. The Conservation Officer had recommended that the group have extra ventilation in the mill and so the Chairman

Dear Mrs Swift

Meir Heath Windmill Preservation Group

10th March 2009

Many thanks for your letter dated 4th March 2009. I am so glad that you found the children's involvement in the design and printing of your flyers a help. I am very interested indeed in your latest venture – the writing of a local history document and would be very pleased to assist wherever possible.

With regard to your request for photos, I attach a CD of photographs compiled by a member of staff, illustrating the old school building and the construction of the new one. I would also like to offer you the opportunity to come and take photographs of the new school now that the landscaping has been completed. You would, however, have to refer to the school as 'Sandon High School'.

Enclosed is a letter of support for the bid you intend to make for grant aid from HLF.

With every good wish. (Enclosed letter)

13th March 2009

Dear Mrs Swift

Sandon High School fully supports the Meir Heath Windmill Preservation Group in writing a local history book about the Meir Heath Windmill and the local area.

The students and teachers at the school have worked with the Preservation Group on a number of projects over a many years to celebrate and promote local history. The Windmill is one of the few local historic buildings in the local facility. There is a strong and enthusiastic history department in school and it is projects like this that bring history alive to students.

The school fully supports the project and would welcome an active involvement in collecting some of the resources for the book and it may be an opportunity for students to interview the elderly on their memories of the local area. This would be of value for community cohesion.

Yours sincerely

Barbara Hall

Head teacher

obtained the ironwork for the grille to be fixed in the door. This was done by Leo Taylor, a joiner. Also at this time, the Chairman took six different builders, drain and guttering suppliers to see the mill and to arrange quotations for work on Phase 2. The Secretary sent off 16 applications for grants to do the work, including waterproof render, aluminium guttering and French drains, but to no avail.

A Night with the Windmill Preservation Society (28 February 2009)

By Joanne Mitchell-Waite

Our evening started at 7.34pm with an introduction to our tent, Midnight Patrol #209. We showed a compilation of clips from all of the Laurel & Hardy films including Laughing Gravy. We then had a raffle prize draw for which we donated a really nice picture frame with Laurel & Hardy postcards and a sweet cigarette wrapper. Joshua then told the room the story about his blue Laurel & Hardy T-shirt, He told them "We went to Amsterdam last year and Stan Laurel's great-granddaughter, Cassidy, gave me my T-shirt." We then watched the third reel of Laughing Gravy. Next we watched You're Darn Tootin'. (I handed out a piece of paper for everyone to rip up when we got to the fabulous trouser-ripping scene, everyone really enjoyed that part!)

We finished the night with Another Fine Mess. What we didn't realise was the time – it was now 9.56pm and we had to vacate by 10.00pm, so it was just like a scene from a Laurel & Hardy film, us rushing about trying to pack up the sales stalls and some of Ant's memorabilia. The next day we received a thank-you email and they told us they made £105.00 profit, which wasn't bad really.

The Committee are grateful for the support given by Antony, Joanne and Josh.

Meir Heath Windmill Preservation Group Meeting at The Windmill Inn (25 February 2011)

Follow-up notes: some extracts from the discussion.

Render

The windmill has recently been pointed in a cementitious mortar. As this is harder than the bricks, this means that rainwater soaks into the bricks rather than the mortar, and in freezing conditions the expansion within the bricks 'blows' the bricks.

It was agreed that there are two solutions to this:

Rake out joints and re-point with a lime mortar: the most painstaking and expensive option.

Reinstate the former lime shelter coat to the whole of the external face of the mill. There is historical evidence that the Windmill was previously either lime-washed, or had a lime 'slurry' shelter coat. John Boucher's report of March 2007 recommended this approach as having 'considerable benefits in moisture proofing'. The current Listed Building Consent includes provision for a lime render and/or lime wash, but a specification needs to be approved. For a breathable waterproofing render, the Borough Conservation Officer (BCO) recommends looking at the 'slurry' approach, which is somewhere between a lime wash and full render, which would achieve waterproofing and would allow the definition of the brick construction to remain evident – a 3-coat sprayed lime render (NHL3.5) is referred to in John Boucher's report and should be worth investigating.

Non-traditional and non-breathable methods of waterproofing the windmill would not gain Listed Building Consent.

Damp-proofing works: Certain measures will assist in drying out the building: Ventilation: the Listed Building Consent covered the circular window being either a fixed or pivot-opening design. The window could be redesigned and replaced if thought essential, but other cheaper options are available. An appropriately designed grille could be inserted into the door, with a mesh behind to prevent litter etc. being thrown into the mill. Airbricks or ceramic pipes could be inserted within the walls. This would need Listed Building Consent. The possibility of opening up what appear to be fireplaces was also discussed – there is no clear evidence of any flue existing in the building, so this would need further investigation.

Rainwater goods: The new boat cap will be throwing rainwater directly onto the cambered walls and saturating them. Guttering and downpipes were provided for in the existing Listed Building Consent (condition 10).

Reinstatement of Sails

Listed Building Consent could only be granted for full accurate reinstatement of the former sails, based on firm historical evidence. This would include, in terms of materials: dimensions, appearance and method of construction. Sails based on hypothetical reconstruction, in alternative materials, or of alternative sizes, would not be supported. The boat cap was not constructed to take the sails, in terms of design or structural capacity. The cap is primarily a method of roofing, which also reinstates the visual appearance of the Victorian cap. Substantial alteration would be necessary to enable sails to be installed. Evidently any sails would impinge on land outside the present curtilage of the mill, and the impact on the car park would need to be taken into consideration. It is agreed that the group's resources are limited and that their aim is to rescue the building from 'risk' and reuse it as a unique education/exhibition room. From a conservation point of view, ensuring the building is in a sustainable condition is the prime consideration. The group agreed to concentrate on dealing with the condition of the mill – i.e. addressing ventilation, drainage and any lime shelter coats – prior to any other more ambitious projects of heritage reconstruction for the mill.

Sponsored Silence Meir Heath Brownies (1950) *(By kind permission of M Flannagan)*

Celebration Party – V Eddows, A Waterfield, W Broom, Cllr E Alison, C Alison and M Wooton *(By kind permission of Sally Barker)*

Mr and Mrs P Herward and granddaughter Lucy with Anthony Swift
in the Windmill – Mrs Herward helps the group when they need to hire
the Rough Close & Meir Heath Village Hall for dances and events

Opening the new Village Hall –
Cllr B Shaw and Mrs Shaw, Cllr E Bevan and Mrs Bevan
(By kind permission of Cllr B Shaw)

Meir Heath Bowling Club – C Wood, V Warren,
R Edge, D Edge, K Wood and M Wood

R Williams (Head teacher, Meir Heath School), B Arrowsmith,
D Dodson, A Williams, A Fox, O Maddox and T Merrideth

Guides and Brownies 1948/9 Review – Information kindly given by A Saville (Colclough) – Brown Owl N Wilcock, Guide Leader J Nixon, S and
C Hammersley, P and H Kiterage, S Birks, O and J Latham, M Jones, I Keeling, P Leese, O Philips, J Hughes, C Rowley, A Smith and H Hughes

M Fox and the bowling team

J Calcott, J Cooke, A Fox, D Cooke, G Harnett and K Harvey
(By kind permission of M Fox)

Women's Institute 50th Birthday Celebrations (2009)

Minutes of the First Meeting 1929
A public meeting was held in Rough Close School on Tuesday April 23rd at 4.15 p.m. to discuss the formation of a Women's Institute in the district of Rough Close.
Twenty-five persons were present at the meeting.

Address by Miss Strachan

Miss Strachan, County Secretary of the Federation of Women's Institutes gave an address on the aims and conduct of the Institute. She discussed:
1. Methods of procuring funds for immediate necessities, when such arose, by holding jumble sales, dances, plays and sales of work.
2. The educational needs of the Institute, which would be supplied by lectures, demonstrations, classes etc.
3. The social amenities of the Institute to be supplied in the form of plays, music, readings of prose and poetry, games and tea.

Formation of the Institute
It was then proposed by Mrs. Leason and seconded by Mrs. Wooliscroft that such an Institute should be formed. All present at the meeting agreed.

Programme for 1947

Jan. 21st - "The law, the parent and the child"   By Mr. Howard
                        Social Half Hour ....Roll Call

Feb. 18th — "This and that in W.I.'s" by Mrs. R.G. Edwards
                    Lucky 6d. Dip ...... Social Half Hour .... Music

Mar. 18th — "Smocking".......................................by Mrs. M.L. Beswick
                    Competition ...Home-made Handkerchief
                    Social Half Hour ....Game

April 15th — "Norway" ....by Miss O.M. Wilkinson, B.A.
                    Bring and buy .... Social Half Hour
                    Play .... Reading

May 20th — "Weaving" ....by Mr. R. Fletcher
                    Competition ....Spring Button-hole
                    Social Half Hour ....Impromptu Speech—2 mins.

June 17th — Open Meeting (Husbands invited)

July 15th — "Local Village History"
                    Competition .... Ginger Biscuits
                    Social Half Hour ...... Music

Sept. 16th — "Stool-Seating"
                    Competition .... Hand Knitted Gloves

Oct. 21st — "German Customs" .... by Mr. R. Gibbons.
                    Bring and Buy .... Social Half Hour ..... Music

Nov. 18th — "Musical appreciation" .... by Mrs. Davenport.
                    Competition .... Xmas Novelty (for sale)
                    Social Half Hour ...... Play .... Reading

Dec. 16th — Election of Officers and Committee for 1948

Mrs K Wildblood, County Chairperson; Mrs E Humpherson, President Rough Close & Meir Heath W.I.; and Mrs M Fox, Secretary *(By kind permission of M Fox)*

W.I. 1929–2009 Rough Close & Meir Heath Branch made the wall hanging which can be seen in the village hall *(By kind permission of M Fox)*

The work begins on Rough Close and Meir Heath Village Hall – B Austin, M Fox, B Mountford, E Bevan, S Warren, M Powell, B Shaw, D Swindale, W Statham, K Allen, A Fox and R Powell
(By kind permission of B Shaw)

The School's Connection

MEIR HEATH PRIMARY SCHOOL
GOLBORN AVENUE
MEIR HEATH
5th April 1977
To the Chairman of the Meir Heath Silver Jubilee Committee.

Dear Sir,

I am sorry that I will not be able to attend this meeting as I shall be in Wales for the week but I have attached a copy of the conditions required for the hiring of the premises. The conditions are very stringent and someone will have to accept the overall responsibility for the hiring. I have drawn up the following points for your guidance:-

Condition A) The local body represented by our school managers are not agreeable to the premises being used for an 'It's a Knockout' type of competition. The Chairman feels in view of the sports on the following day that excessive wear may be caused to the pitch. He also feels that undesirable elements of the local population may be attracted to the premises. The general feeling among the managers was that the using of the school field, toilets, canteen and two classrooms for a sports event during Monday was a perfectly reasonable and acceptable request. They have considerable reservations about the further use of the school on that day for the purpose of a dance.

Condition B) No school furniture can be used outside on the field. This includes chairs and tables. PE equipment will be available for the sports providing the hiring body are prepared to make good any damage or losses. A public address system has been booked.

Condition C) The canteen may only be used for preparation of hot drinks and washing up. No food can be prepared in this room. A member of the canteen staff must be on paid duty throughout the letting. Whoever signs the application form will be held responsible for the cost of any damage to the grounds or fabric of the school building. I hope you will appreciate that these regulations are laid down by the Local Education Authority and it is my duty to see that they are adhered to. Mrs Nixon is in a similar position in the School Canteen and to ask her to waive any regulations that might lead to disciplinary action being taken against her would be most unfair. Mr Follows, the school caretaker, has a previous commitment on that day and cannot be asked to work as it is a Public Bank Holiday. I am prepared to accept responsibility for opening and locking the premises from 10 to 6 but would be unable to take on the duty at night. A suitable responsible person would have to be nominated for this duty.

Yours sincerely, J Fisher

Meir Heath and Rough Close Village Hall Committee (Sept 1975–Sept 1976)				
Association	**Nominated Representatives**	**Address**	**Telephone**	**Sub-Committee**
Cricket Club	Mr R Rhead	'Field View' Hilderstone Rd Meir Heath	Blythe Bridge 3629	Land – 5
Women's Institute	Mrs H Green	Yew Tree Cottage Grindley Lane Meir Heath	Blythe Bridge 3428	Funds – 4
Rough Close Social Club	Mr P Banting	The Gables Church Close Meir Heath	Blythe Bridge 3065	Land – 9
Meir Heath Social Club (Lads & Dads)	Mr J Bromley (Chairman)	40 Pemberton Drive Meir Heath	Blythe Bridge 3589	Social – 3
Scouts & Cubs	Mrs S Devine	45 Blythe Avenue Meir Heath	Blythe Bridge 3226	Social
Music – Art Society	Declined to be Represented			
Good Companions	Mr F Harold	43 Hollies Drive Meir Heath	-	Social
Play Group	Mrs M Flannagon	3 Birkholme Drive Meir Heath	Blythe Bridge 3846	Funds – 2
Men's Club				6
Mothers' Union	Mrs J Tooth	1 Birch Grove Meir Heath	Blythe Bridge 4714	Funds – 7
Parents & Teachers Association	Mrs V Nixon	38 Pemberton Drive Meir Heath	-	Social – 1
County Education Committee				
General Public	Mr A Whitfield	38 Blythe Avenue Meir Heath	Blythe Bridge 6330	Social
-	Mr A Walker	7 Grindley Lane Meir Heath	Blythe Bridge 3678	Funds
-	Mrs B Mountford	34 Grindley Lane Meir Heath	-	Social
-	Mr A Fox (Treasurer)	50 Blythe Avenue Meir Heath	Blythe Bridge 4838	Funds
-	Mr E Smith (Secretary)	29 Pemberton Drive Meir Heath	Blythe Bridge 4842	Land
-	Mr S Bath	56 Blythe Avenue Meir Heath	-	Land
-	Mr R Edwards	29 Birkholme Drive Meir Heath	Blythe Bridge 3098	Funds
--	Mrs S Wheat	5 Blythe Avenue Meir Heath	Blythe Bridge 7753	Social
	Mr G Degg	1 Golborn Avenue Meir Heath	Blythe Bridge 2807	Land

Townswomen's Guild

Patron HRH Princess Anne Information from Mary Flannagan

Our Guild is in its eleventh year, but the Townswomen's guild began 80 years ago.

In 1928, after years of bitter struggle, women were granted full voting rights. Now that the right to vote had been achieved, women could look to the future.

Eva Hubback, Parliamentary Secretary for the women's suffrage movement, was in hospital when Margaret Corbett Ashby went to visit her. They were inspired by leading suffragist Dame Millicent Fawcett, who urged her colleagues to go forward and educate the 'new citizens'.

Mrs Corbett Ashby and others recognised that as new housing estates were built and the growth of suburbs began after the 1914–18 war, there was a need for somewhere for women to meet and take part in activities and develop new interests.

In villages neighbours knew each other, but in the suburbs, young wives could live for years without getting to know their neighbours. From this came the proposal to form societies in towns for all women, regardless of their creed or party. Their slogan was 'After the vote, the education of the woman'. On 23 January 1929, the first Townswomen's institute was formed at Hayward's Heath in Sussex. Many more quickly followed. In 2004, there were approximately 55,000 members and 1,200 guilds throughout the United Kingdom. Townswomen's members are encouraged to have ideas and views, develop new skills, campaign on various issues, support each other, make new friends and, above all, have fun! Our Guild meets at the Meir Heath and Rough Close Village Hall once a month. We have a small committee which meets monthly to organise activities and speakers. We have a varied programme of speakers from all walks of life who deliver talks on history, travel, fashion, crafts, cookery and careers to name but a few. Our afternoon ends with the obligatory tea and biscuits and a chat with friends. We have an annual outing, birthday party and Christmas meal.

Meir Heath in the 1950s to 1960s

Sheila Mason, Carnival Queen

There was a lovely photograph in the Sentinel newspaper of what looked like a carnival but no one I asked knew who the people were. In the Sentinel, Colette Warbrook has a section called 'The Way We Were' and it has photographs and letters from people in the area. Thinking someone might see my photographs in Colette's column, I sent a letter to her asking for help. Sure enough, on 25 February 2012, the photos appeared in the newspaper. On Saturday 25 February, at 9.30am, the phone rang and a lady called Honra Hughes (Mrs Shirley) spoke to me. She knew most of the people in the photograph. Later that day and the next day, eight people rang to confirm what Honra had told me.

On Wednesday that week, David Mason rang and told me that his sister, Sheila Mason, had been the Carnival Queen. Later that evening, at about 9.30pm, the phone rang and it was David's niece, Sally Barker, who was thrilled to know the photograph had been in the Sentinel. Sally lives in Cambridge and her uncle, David Mason, had rung to tell her of my research. On Thursday morning I was pleased to receive an email with seven photographs of people at the carnival and people in St Francis Snooker Hall and at a Christmas Show, and also one of the Guides and Brownies. Sally sent me all the details about her mother, Sheila Mason (Smith), who had been Meir Heath Carnival Queen and later Carnival Queen of Great Britain. Mr Stewart Holmes, the bearer of the crown, rang to tell me that he had spoken to his sister Diane. The night before, Diane had rung to say that the little girl at the front was certainly her; she had a plaster on her leg. When Sally and her family come to visit the Potteries, we are going to meet at the Windmill. I am grateful to Sally and the family for their help.

Mrs Walker's daughter rang to say that she and her mother, Mrs J Walker, knew many people in the photograph and that the carnival had been 'opened' by her grandfather, Councillor Leonard Evans. Mr Ray Williamson rang and he could tell me about the other photograph with Councillor Eddie Allison in it. Mr Williamson now lives in Stone, but used to live in Meir Heath when his father was the local policeman. Also thanks to Mrs I Hewitt, Mrs J Walker and to the other lady who left a message.

The Carnival Queen and friends taken on the field at Hilderstone Road – Sheila Mason, Honra Hughes, Rosemarie Mason, Christine Wooton, Rosemary Burton, Ada Evans, Janet Stuart and Diane Holmes *(By kind permission of Sally Barker)*

The 21st birthday party of David Mason (3 June 1952) – David Mason in the middle of the photo (bow tie), Mr and Mrs Mason, and family and friends *(By kind permission of David Mason and Sally Barker)*

Extra Facts About the 1770s

We know that the windmill would have been whirling at the time of Waterloo and probably at the time the Duke of Wellington had his victory over Napoleon.

Carnival Queen Sheila Mason (Meir Heath Carnival)
(By kind permission Sally Barker)

Meir Park – Interesting Street Names

Fennel, Tarragon Chervil, Alderton, Picasso, Rubens, Constable, Partridge, Quail, Plover, Falcon, Kestrel, Sperry, Wenham, Romford, Kingsnorth, Glaisher, Farnborough, Lysander, Brabazon, Canberra, Bleriot, Hermes, Halifax.

The first names, as you will notice, are names of herbs. There are a few names of famous artists and birds but the ones that are really special are the last list.

Lord Brabazon of Tara 1884–1964

John Moore-Brabazon

In Memoriam

Lord Brabazon of Tara was born in England on 8 February 1884 and died in London on 17 May 1964. He first soloed in a French Voisin biplane at Issy-les-Montineaux, France, in 1908.

French F.A.I. (Federation Aeronautique Internationale) brevet# 40 was issued to him under the name of Brabazon Moore, on 8 March 1910, before he became a member of the House of Lords in England.

British F.A.I. Aeroplane Pilot's Certificate Number 1 was issued to him by the Royal Aero Club, making him the first person to be licensed in Great Britain as an Aeroplane Pilot.

In 1909 he made the first live cargo flight by aeroplane, by tying a waste paper basket to a wing-strut of his Voisin aeroplane. Then, using it as a cargo hold, he lifted one small pig.

In October of that year, Mr Moore-Brabazon won the first all-British competition of £1,000 offered by the Daily Mail for the first plane to fly a circular mile course. His plane was fitted with a 60-horsepower Green aeroengine. In the same year, M. Michelin offered a £1,000 prize for a long-distance flight. This was also won by Mr Brabazon, flying for 17 miles.

George III (1738 - 1820)

George III was the third Hanoverian king of Great Britain. During his reign, Britain lost its American colonies but emerged as a leading power in Europe. He suffered from recurrent fits of madness and after 1810, his son acted as regent.

George III was born on 4 June 1738 in London, son of Frederick, Prince of Wales and Augusta of Saxe-Gotha. He became heir to the throne when his father died in 1751, succeeding his grandfather George II in 1760. He was the first Hanoverian monarch to use English as his first language. In 1761, George married Charlotte of Mecklenburg-Strelitz and they enjoyed a happy marriage, with 15 children.

George chose his mentor the Earl of Bute as his first chief minister. He was a poor cho from senior politicians. Effective government became almost impossible, and George v vilified. The instability following Bute's resignation in 1763 did little to solve the crown difficulties, made worse by the Seven Years' War. In 1770, George appointed Lord No minister. Although an effective administrator, North's government was dominated by the American colonists over British attempts to levy taxes on them. War began in 177 in 1779, at the king's insistence, to prevent copycat protests elsewhere. The British de prompted North to resign.

In 1783, North and the prominent Whig politician Fox formed a coalition government. reform the East India Company gave George the chance to regain popularity. He force Parliament, and the two resigned. In their place George appointed William Pitt the You combination of Pitt's skill and war with France in 1793 strengthened George's position over emancipation of the Catholics - Pitt was in favour and George vehemently oppose resignation in 1801.

The American war, its political aftermath and family quarrels put great strain on Georg bouts of illness in 1788 - 1789 and 1801, thought now to be caused by porphyria, he deranged in 1810. The Prince of Wales (later George IV) became regent.

George remained ill until his death at Windsor Castle on 29 January 1820. In 1801, ur Great Britain and Ireland were united into a single nation - the United Kingdom. Geor

LICENSING ACT, 1964.

Grant of Occasional Licence

In exercise of *our powers under section 180 of the Licensing Act 1964 as amended by the Finance Act 1967, **WE** the undersigned Justices of the Peace sitting at

.   the Court House, Stone

HEREBY GRANT to   Mr. J.A. Castles

of

.   Windmill Inn, Meir Heath

being the [[personal representative] [trustee] of the] holder of a justices on-licence] [person granted a protection order] in respect of premises known as †

.   Windmill Inn

this occasional licence authorising h im   to sell ‡ [intoxicating liquor of al descriptions] [[beer] [and] [cider] [and] [wine] only] [on the   19th

day   of   March   19 76] [during the period from the day of   19   , to the

.   day of   19] between the

hours of   8.00 p.m.   and   11.30 p.m.   , at §   Primary School situated at

.   Meir Heath

on the occasion of a

DATED this   10th   day of   March   19 76

Justices of the Peace

NOTES.

1.   This licence must be produced on demand to a Justice of the Peace or constable.

2.   If the holder of this licence is authorised to sell spirits, he must, when he sends out spirits from his stock at his licensed premises to the place of occasional sale, prepare a spirits consignment note which may be retained at his licensed premises. It must be produced there to an Officer of Customs and Excise on request at any time during the next twelve months.

3.   Directions governing the preparation and retention of spirits consignment notes are contained in Customs and Excise Notice No. 62 a copy of which may be obtained from any Customs and Excise office.

* Where the circumstances are such that a single justice may exercise powers conferred by section 199

You Shop Online – They Give to our Charity

Our group tried to raise extra funds by using the site set up by the Giving Machine. We produced the following leaflet.

Can you use this when buying goods online? Donate to the Meir Heath Windmill Preservation Group.

Dear Sir/Madam, Please shop online and help the Windmill Project.

THE GIVING MACHINE is only available to help charitable groups.

It helps to create revenue for the group and is free to both charity and shoppers.

It is connected to online shopping and is a great site with widest selection of recognised online brands. Every giver who registers with THE GIVING MACHINE creates an account that includes the charity they wish to support (Meir Heath Windmill Preservation Group). The site enables online shoppers to click to their favourite retailers. Every purchase they make automatically pays a donation of 5% of the total bill to the good cause. We need the support from businesses and from the public in order to create the unique Heritage Centre for us all and for future generations to enjoy. If you can help, please contact the Secretary Mrs Gill Swift 01782 317521 or Mrs D Bestwick Treasurer 01782 392419.

Windmill Memorable Moments for Gill & Tony Swift

The problem is where to start because there have been so many memorable moments. Vivid memories keep flooding back. In August 2006, Gill slipped on the stairs at home and broke her left leg. In plaster and feeling very low in spirits, the day brightened when the post arrived. In spite of the broken leg, she tried to dance, for on 11 August 2006 the group became a charity and Company Limited by Guarantee

Our group is really indebted to Terry Walsh (Presenter Good Times Radio Stoke).

And to Ian White (Solicitor, Knights). We were being interviewed on Radio Stoke, appealing for a solicitor to help us obtain the lease to the windmill. The memorable moment was when Ian White heard us and rang in to offer his services.

To raise money for the project, we held a series of meetings and Steve Birks (potteries org), historian, came to visit. His evening became known to all as Chocolate evening because Steve loves Jaffa cakes, and so we decided that we would all eat chocolate during his visit. It's become a tradition.

A friend of ours is a Rotarian and he invited us to go and inform the Blythe Bridge members about the work done to the windmill. This function was at the Upper House, Barlaston, and included dinner there. An enthusiastic audience enjoyed the evening.

In the summer we hold a dog show and fair at the windmill, and have Heather Gordon (judge, trainer) and Bruce Barker (Rogers Brock Barker vets) to guide us. A memorable moment that caused much amusement was when the nurse had the dogs to examine. As we approached the gazebo, the nurse was to be seen holding the dog on a table and lifting up its tail to inspect its rear end. The children thought this very funny.

Later that evening, we called at our son's home in Grindley Lane. His first comments were "Hi Mum, I could hear your announcements here! Good speakers they have."

We hadn't realised how good the speakers had been. After being on Radio Stoke, there was another phone call. This time from Beryl Lancaster who had lived next door to Gill in Fenton in the 1940s. Really, to meet again after over 60 years! Beryl is now our model at the fashion shows we have and there are more memorable moments.

Gill's history teacher from Thistley Hough is now one hundred and one years old. Miss G Robinson, or Robbo, is really interested in the project and sent a donation. When Gill rang to thank her, they talked about the Corn Laws.

"As the price of English corn rose to 80 shillings a quarter, more and more foreign corn came into the country." This memorable moment would be shared by all the old girls from Thistley Hough who studied history with Miss Robinson.

There were disappointing moments when we heard that the lottery couldn't help. So many other funders couldn't help either. There were happy memorable moments as well. Laurel and Hardy film shows, visits to schools, getting a red hard hat, having fun with the Sweet Melody Dreamboat Band and Fuzzy Logic Band – they are all remembered.

On a very personal note, we both remember 10 April 2007 when our granddaughter was born early, at 25 weeks premature and only weighing one pound five ounces. That was the most memorable moment of them all. Olivia is now five years of age.

From 2004 to 2012, there are some wonderful memories we share.

LIST OF SUBSCRIBERS

Howard & Linda Platt, Meir Heath, Staffs

Ann Cartlidge, Barlaston, Staffs

Brenda Smith, Blythe Bridge, Staffs

Celia Shemilt, Lightwood, Staffs

Dawn Mason, Lightwood, Staffs

Peter & Carla Mason and baby

Rosemarie Brassington, Dilhorne

Robert Mason, Stone, Staffs

George Mason, Dilhorne, Staffs

June & Tony Lane, Heron Cross, Staffs

Roy Fox, Meir Heath, Staffs

Bill Durose, Endon, Staffs

Sheila E. Allen, Weston Coyney, Staffs

Neil Hopkins, Lightwood, Staffs

J Horsefield, Trentham, Staffs

Roy Deakin, Meir Heath, Staffs

Margaret & Bill Cochrane, Southport

Mary Lewis, Lightwood, Staffs

Patricia Leese, Friars Ave, Stone, Staffs

Mrs Hildred M. Deakin, Stone, Staffs

Kenneth Vincent, Hilderstone Rd, Staffs

Lyn Parmer (nee Deakin) Leics

Mick & Betty Mathers, Meir Heath, Staffs

Roy Lindermere, Meir Heath, Staffs

Mr&Mrs Cotton, Meir Heath, Staffs

Cllr Malcolm Millichap
(Mayor of Stafford 2010-2011)

J Hughes BDS Dentist, Meir Heath, Staffs

Dr M Salt, Meir Heath, Staffs

Di& Bri Halket, Lightwood, Staffs

Tony & Lyn Davis, Australia

Necmi Suricickigil, Turkey

Millicent Howe, Hanley, Staffs

Olivia Mary Swift, Meir Heath, Staffs

Christian Bradbury, Meir Heath, Staffs

William Keeling, Lightwood, Staffs

Mr & Mrs D.L.Swift, Meir Heath, Staffs

John Banks, Yarnfield, Staffs, formerly of MILL HOUSE

John W. Mason,Lightwood ,Staffs

Paul Mason, Fenton, Staffs

Dawn Louise

Alan Mason, Rough Close, Staffs

David Mason, Stone, Staffs

Kathleen & Mike Rogers, Cheddleton, Staffs,

Gladys Massey, Burston, Staffs

John B. Hill, Meir Heath, Staffs

Barry & Maureen Shaw, Meir Heath, Staffs

Mrs Mary Freeman, J.P.Blythe Bridge, Staffs

Peter Lawton, Lightwood ,Staffs

A Sim (Andy's Butchers) Meir Heath, Staffs

David, Rita Oliver & James Deakin, Staffs

R.D. Cresswell, Hilderstone, Staffs

Ruth Taylor, Staffs
(Nee Whitehead in memory of her parents 1933-1979)

Mr Edward Meigh, Clayton, Staffs

Andre & Joanne Hill, Meir Heath, Staffs

Edith & Keith Charsley, May Bank, Staffs

Richard & Edna Durose, Caverswall, Staffs

Pat & Tony Sanders, Meir Park, Staffs

Mrs T Ash, Meir Heath, Staffs

Reg & Sylvia Sweetmore, Meir Heath, Staffs

Mrs Mellony Millichap
(Mayoress of Stafford, 2010-2011)

Margaret Webb, Blurton, Staffs

David & Sharon, Beardmore, Clayton, Staffs

Celia & Barry Unett, Stafford

Hellen & Maurice Riley, Australia

Susan &R oyston Cooke, Werrington, Staffs

Pat Swift, Meir Park, Staffs

Robyn Bradbury, Meir Heath, Staffs

Jane Brownridge, Newcastle, Staffs

Hilary Baxter, Alsager, Staffs

Paul Philpott, Barlaston, Staffs

Dorothy Bestwick, Meir Park, Staffs

Mary Flannagan, Meir Heath, Staffs

Quinton & Cath Cartlidge, London

Doreen & Roy Fraser, Dorset

Lyn Hollins , Wolverhampton

Di & Peter Harvey, Yarnfield, Staffs

Wendy & Ken Jones, Stone, Staffs

Irene Homer, Cradely Heath, Staffs

Margaret Leech, Meir Heath, Staffs

Dr P. Martin, Worthing

Maralyn Brindley, Blythe Bridge, Staffs

Pat Middleton, Lightwood, Staffs

Nathan Philpott, London

S Wardill, Bridlington, Yorks

Rebecca & Ryan Cartlidge, Cardiff, Wales

Kate Unett, Walton-on Hill, Staffs

(Windmill Inn) now Llandudno

Harvey Swetnam, Meir Heath, Staffs

Colin & Cath Shaw, Meir Heath, Staffs

Norma & Derek Walker, Blythe Bridge, Staffs

Terry Brereton Meir Heath, Staffs

Bob & Ann Evans, Meir Heath, Staffs

Jacqueline Walker, Weston Coyney, Staffs

J Hirst, Hilderstone Road, Staffs

Jean Royle, Kidsgrove, Staffs

Rowena Dawson, Meir Heath, Staffs

George Howard, Stoke, Staffs

Basil Gordon Blythe Bridge, Staffs

Janet & David Swindail, Meir Heath, Staffs

James, Kathy, Eli, Angus, Ezra & Mac Darley

S Mclauclan, Meir Heath, Staffs

Cath Pointon, Meir Heath, Staffs

Cllr Elaine Philpott, Barlaston, Staff

Beryl Lancaster, Newchaple, Staffs

Thomas Bestwick, Lightwood, Staffs

Emma Khaleefa (Nee Flannagan) & Zara Khaleefa

Ann Elesmore, Sambourne

Roger Green, Derbyshire

Mary & Peter Burrows, Blurton, Staffs

Eileen Hallam, Meir, Staffs

Josephine Swift, Oswestry, Salop

Kay Walker, Meir, Staffs

Dr Viv Martin, Worthing

Christopher Mason, Bournemouth, Hants

Clive & Nita Mould, Barlaston, Staffs

Alfred Oakes, Meir Heath, Staffs

G Robinson, Bridlington, Yorks

Jean Royle, Kidsgrove, Staffs

Joanne Unett, Stafford

Julia Jackson (nee Gimbert)

Rita Jones, Bagnall Staffs (worked at the Windmill Inn)

Shirley Evans, Rough Close, Staffs

Sheila Sargeant, Meir Heath, Staffs

Nigel Karen & Robert Morley, Draycot, Staffs

Joan &Winston Hathaway, Meir Heath, Staffs

Peter Wood, Meir Heath, Staffs

Dorothy Mear, Trent Vale, Staffs

Christine Stanier, Meir Heath, Staffs

Pauline Marsden, Sandon Business Colledge

Stewart Sim, Stafford

Paul Howard, Stoke Staffs

Robert J Waterfall, Meir Heath, Staffs

David Mason, Meir Heath, Staffs

Barrie Roberts, Meir Park, Staffs

A Mountford, Meir Heath, Staffs

NOTES

NOTES

BEHOLD A GIANT *The Story of a Windmill*